TABLE SAW BENCH GUIDE

Roger W. Cliffe

STERLING PUBLISHING CO. INC., NEW YORK

10 9 8 7 6 5 4 3

Series Editor: Michael Cea
Series Designer: Chris Swirnoff

Published 2002 by Sterling Publishing Company, Inc.
387 Park Avenue South, New York, New York 10016
Originally published under the title *Table Saw: Workshop Bench reference*
© 1999 by Roger W. Cliffe
Distributed in Canada by Sterling Publishing
C/o Canadian Manda Group, One Atlantic Avenue, Suite 105
Toronto, Ontario, Canada M6K 3E7
Distributed in Great Britain by Chrysalis Books
64 Brewery Road, London N7 9NT, England
Distributed in Australia by Capricorn Link (Australia) Pty. Ltd.
P.O. Box 704, Windsor, NSW 2756 Australia
Printed in China

Sterling ISBN 0-8069-9135-6

Dedication

During the time it took to complete this book, I lost two special friends. Donna Ponne Wold had planned to do all of the line drawings for this book. She was taken by cancer after completing just a few. While I was putting the finishing touches on this book, her spouse and my friend, Wallace Palmer Wold, died suddenly.

I have enjoyed many pleasant times with these two special people. They were friends, artists, and helpers to all. I miss them both. I dedicate this book to them—two people who were able to live their dream.

Acknowlegments

I would like to acknowledge the help of camera assistants Jim Schmidtz and Zach Rouse. Thanks also to darkroom expert Laura Christerson, who made the photographs even better.

In the power-tool area, I would like to thank Delta International Machinery Corporation for its assistance with photographs. Some of the line drawings came from table-saw manuals; thanks to Sil Argentin from Skil-Bosch Power Tools and Mike Mangan from Sears Craftsman.

Many thanks for your help!

Credits
The information in the Troubleshooting Guidelines table on pages 35 and 36 courtesy of Jesada Tools and Skil Power Tools.

Contents

Introduction

The table saw is a stationary wood-cutting tool. It is most commonly used for cutting wood with the grain (ripping); cutting wood across the grain (crosscutting); or cutting wood at an angle (mitering or beveling). In addition to these common cuts, the table saw can be used to make joinery such as dadoes (U-shaped channels in wood) and rabbets (L-shaped channels along the edge or end of a workpiece).

This book describes and illustrates how to perform these techniques and many more. It is

Author Roger Cliffe

written for table-saw users at all levels of expertise, ranging from those totally unfamiliar with the tool to experts looking to perform an advanced technique safely and effectively. It details the table saw's different components and accessories and describes maintenance and troubleshooting techniques; instructs on how to select and use saw blades and dado heads to perform an array of tasks when cutting wood and non-wood materials; and describes door-making, sanding, and molding techniques. Observe the safety techniques described with each operation. Pay particular attention to the safety techniques emphasized in Chapter 10.

The information in the following pages is easily accessible. Specific information can be found by referring to the Contents pages, the tabs and chapter openings, or the index. The glossary will also prove to be a valuable tool in clarifying terms and referring the reader to pertinent information. No matter which approach is taken, the reader will find in the following pages ways to make the table saw a more productive, efficient, and safer workshop companion

1 Components and Features

Types of Table Saw

There are two general types of table saw: motorized and motor-driven. Understanding the difference will help you select the best saw for the job. *Motorized table saws* have no belts between the motor and blade. The blade is attached to the end of the motor (1–1). The motor used on a motorized table saw is usually the universal type. It turns at higher revolutions per minute and is generally noisier than a motor-driven table saw. Most benchtop table saws are motorized. This

1–1. *This motorized saw has a universal motor. The blade is mounted to the arbor, which is actually the end of the motor.*

allows the operator to use more of the blade above the table. The motor is designed to use a minimum of space under the table. On a job site, lighter, portable motorized table saws with less horsepower should be used. In the shop, heavier motorized table saws with more horsepower are used.

Motor-driven table saws use induction motors (motors designed to operate only on alternating currents) and deliver power to the saw arbor (the metal shaft on the table saw on which the circular-saw blade is mounted; refer to 1–24) using one or more belts (1–2). The belts transfer power from the motor to the blade. The motor on motor-driven table saws may be suspended under the table or behind the table. Another style of motor-driven saw uses a flexible cable to transfer power from the motor to the blade. Table saws with this drive style are not currently

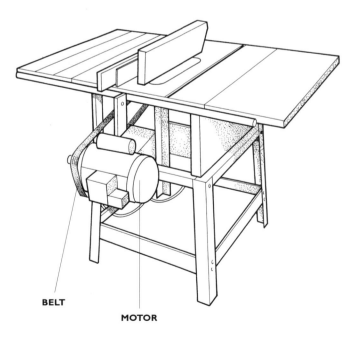

BELT

MOTOR

1–2. Motor-driven saws use induction motors. A belt or series of belts from the motor to the arbor drive the arbor and the blade.

in production. Flexible cables do not generate vibration, but they may generate more noise than a belt or series of belts. Belts, when aligned properly, will produce little vibration.

There are three general types of motorized or motor-driven table saw: *benchtop, or variety, saws*; *contractor saws*; and *cabinet saws*. Benchtop table saws get their name from their compact size. In most cases, they are designed to sit on a bench or pair of sawhorses (1–3), but an accessory stand may be available for some models. The chief advantage of the bench saw is its portability. The small, light saw can be stored in an area that does not take up much space. The chief disadvantage of the bench saw is its table size. Its table is much smaller than the table on a contractor or cabinet saw. There is very little table on the infeed side of the blade. This makes the handling of large pieces more difficult.

Contractor table saws are found in the shop and on some jobs. The contractor saw is motor-driven and has a large table, which is usually made of cast iron or some die-cast metal, usually aluminum (1–4). The contractor saw may run on 110 or 220 volts A.C. The 220-volt models are usually found in workshops, because they are less likely to bog down during a heavy cut. Contractor saws are usually sold with a stand.

Most contractor saws have a motor that extends from the back of the saw (refer to 1–2), although, in some cases, the motor is housed under the table. When the motor extends from the back of the saw, it is more difficult to collect sawdust. The chief advantage of the contractor saw is its moderate price. The saw is extremely versatile for its price. The chief disadvantage is that the saw is difficult to adjust if it becomes misaligned. This is because the elevating-and-tilting mechanism (trunnion) is attached to the underside of the table.

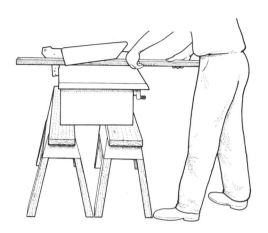

1–3. This bench saw is motorized. It is easy to move on the job site because it is small and lightweight. The saw is clamped to a pair of sawhorses or other stand for use on the job site.

1–4. Contractor saws, which are generally found in workshops, are motor-driven and have large tables usually made of cast iron or die-cast metal. (Photo courtesy of Jet International Machinery Corporation.)

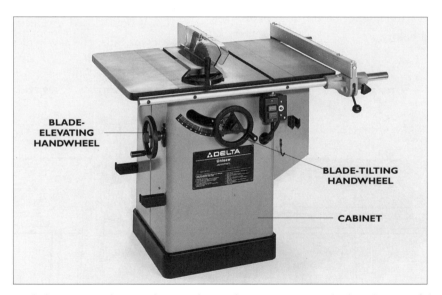

BLADE-
ELEVATING
HANDWHEEL

BLADE-TILTING
HANDWHEEL

CABINET

1–5. The blade-tilting-and-elevating mechanism (trunnion) on cabinet saws is attached to the top of the cabinet. Alignment is simply a matter of loosening and turning the table slightly. (Photo courtesy of Delta International Machinery.)

Cabinet saws are found in larger production shops (1–5). The cabinet saw gets its name from the metal cabinet that contains the saw. It extends from the floor to the underside of the table. The trunnion, or elevating-and-tilting mechanism, is mounted to the cabinet rather than the underside of the table. Cabinet saws usually have higher horsepower than contractor saws and always operate on 220 volts.

The chief advantages of using cabinet saws are ease of adjustment and alignment. To realign the saw, only the top has to be moved. Because of the cabinet, sawdust collection is much easier; in fact, many cabinet saws have dust-collection hookups built into the cabinet. The chief disadvantage to the cabinet saw is its cost. Also, it is much heavier than bench or contractor saws and is suited only for the shop.

It should be noted that some current contractor saws have a full cabinet base, but they are not a true cabinet saw since the trunnion is mounted to the underside of the table. These contractor saws are more difficult to align than any true cabinet saw.

Components

There are several standard components common to all types of table saw (1–6). These are the controls, guard, miter gauge, fence, and throat plate. Each is described below.

CONTROLS

The three common controls on all table saws are the power switch, the blade-elevating handwheel, and the blade-tilting handwheel.

Power Switch

The power switch on most contractor and bench table saws consists of a keyed flip switch. When the key portion is removed, the saw cannot be turned on (1–7). This feature prevents access to the saw by unauthorized operators; it is an important feature when the saw is in a home where children live or visit.

Cabinet saws usually have a magnetic starting switch. This type of switch reduces the voltage (and shock hazard) present at the switch. The switch is held closed by electromagnetic force. If the power fails, the saw will go off and will not

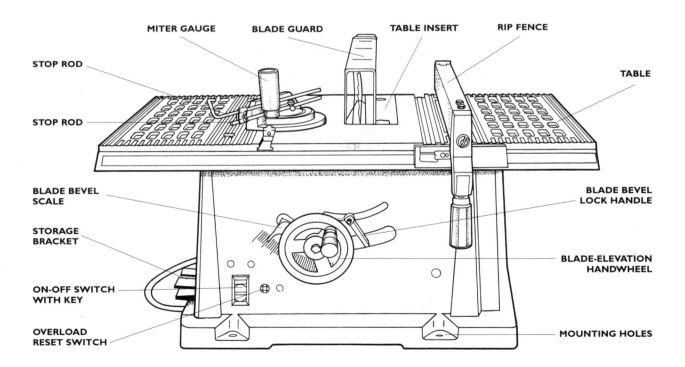

1–6. *The components common to all types of table saws are the controls, guard, fence, miter gauge, and throat plate. (Drawing courtesy of Sears Craftsman.)*

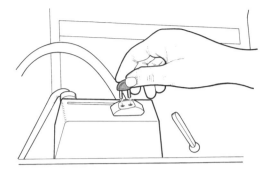

1–7. Many power switches have a key in them. The key can prevent unauthorized operators from using the saw.

start again when the power is restored. The switch must be turned on again. This safety feature eliminates injury from accidental restart. Most *bench* and *contractor* saws do not have this feature.

In addition to the power switch, many table saws are equipped with thermal overload protection (1–8). This is a thermal switch that opens if the motor becomes hot from hard use or abuse. The switch cannot be closed until the motor cools. Reset buttons are found on the motor or

1–8. The thermal overload protection switch, a feature found on many table saws, prevents the motor from overheating. Note the reset button to the right of the switch. This illustration shows the operator tightening the blade's tilt-lock lever, discussed on page 18. This is done after he has determined the desired angle of cut. The scale on the front of the saw indicates the approximate angle.

near the power switch. *Caution: Be certain that the power switch is in the "off" position and that nothing is touching the blade before resetting the thermal overload switch.*

Blade-Elevating Handwheel

When the blade-elevating handwheel is turned, the gear mechanism raises or lowers the saw blade. On most saws, the blade is raised when the blade is turned clockwise. Become familiar with the elevating mechanism; learn how much the blade is elevated in one revolution of the handwheel. This information will make adjustments easier. For example, if one revolution raises the blade ½ inch, a quarter-revolution will raise it ⅛ inch.

Most elevating mechanisms have a locking device to hold the setting (1–9). It is usually in the center of the handwheel, but it may be a ring or level behind the handwheel. Be sure the locking device is loosened before making any adjustments. For accurate adjustment of blade height, it is best to make the final adjustment by raising the blade. This will remove any slack in the mechanism and hold the setting once the locking device is actuated.

1–9. Turning the knob in the middle of the blade-elevating handwheel locks the blade elevation on many saws.

Blade-Tilting Handwheel

The blade-tilting handwheel controls the tilt of the blade on some saws. On other saws, the unit is tilted by loosening the blade-tilt lock lever (refer to 1–8). There is usually a scale on the front of the saw that indicates the approximate blade angle. For very precise settings, it is best to measure the angle between the blade and the table (1–10). There are usually positive stops on the tilting mechanism at 45 and 90 degrees. These stops may require adjustment. Always check the angles before you begin sawing. On some table saws, the blade angle is set by loosening a lock lever and using the blade-elevating handwheel to set the angle (1–11 and 1–12).

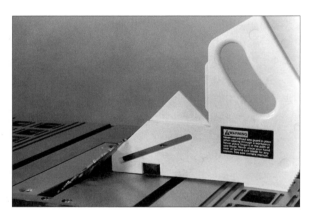

1–10. Precision measuring guides ensure an accurate setting at the desired angle. Keep the measuring device on the plate of the blade for accurate settings.

GUARD

The guard acts as a barrier between the operator and the blade. A table-saw guard consists of three parts: the splitter, or spreader; the anti-kickback pawls; and a barrier (1–13). When rip cuts are made, the splitter and anti-kickback pawls must be used. The splitter keeps the kerf (opening made by the blade) open. The anti-kickback pawls ride on the wood. If the workpiece is

SETTING BLADE ANGLE

1–11. On some table saws, such as this bench saw, setting the blade angle consists of first releasing the lock lever.

1–12. Then the elevating handwheel is pushed in to engage the tilting mechanism. Once the blade is in position, the clamp is locked again. The elevating handwheel is pulled out to adjust blade height.

thrown back at the operator, the anti-kickback pawls would dig into the wood and stop the movement (1–14). The anti-kickback pawls are a one-way device. Wood can only travel away from the operator when they are in use. The splitter and anti-kickback pawls do not have to be used when a crosscut is made, but with some guards the splitter and anti-kickback pawls are actually part of the barrier, so they are in use for all cuts where the guard is used (1–15).

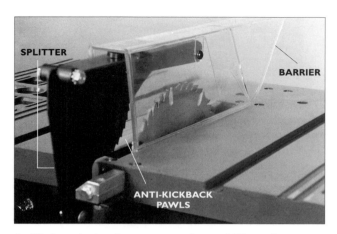

1–13. A typical splitter-mounted guard. The splitter attaches to the saw, and the barrier and anti-kickback pawls are attached to the splitter.

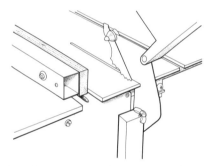

1–14. The splitter, or spreader, prevents the saw kerf from closing on the blade. The anti-kickback pawls ride on the wood. If the wood starts to kick back, the pawls dig into the wood.

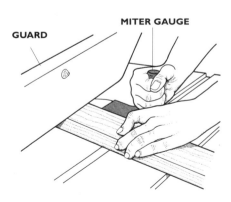

1–15. The splitter-mounted guard employs the splitter and anti-kickback pawls, even on crosscuts and miter cuts.

Splitter-Mounted Guard

Since most table-saw operations are through cuts (cuts that separate the stock into two pieces), the splitter-mounted guard is the most common type of guard in use. The splitter-mounted guard is mounted to a bracket immediately behind the blade and lower than the table surface. This splitter attaches to the bracket and is aligned with the blade. The splitter supports the anti-kickback pawls and the barrier portion of the guard.

Since the splitter is always in the blade path, the guard cannot work if the cut does not separate the wood into two pieces. The splitter stops the wood. A thin-kerf blade will cause a similar problem if not precisely aligned. The smaller cut or kerf in the wood will not clear the splitter. For some non-through cuts, such as rabbets or tenons, the guard must be removed to make the cut. Only experienced operators should do cuts made with the guard removed. When a guard is removed, work accessories such as jigs, push sticks, and featherboards should be used to control stock and keep hands clear of the saw blade (1–16). Always replace the guard when the cut is complete.

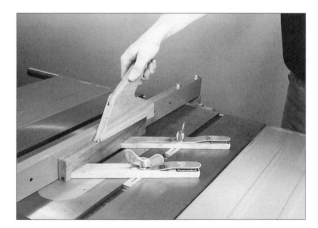

1–16. When the stock is not separated into two parts, a splitter-mounted guard cannot be used. A push stick and featherboards make this cut safer.

1–17. The overarm guard is suspended above the blade. The two sides of the guard work independently. This adds to the versatility of the guard. (Photo courtesy of Delta International Machinery Corporation.)

Overarm Guard

Overarm guards differ from splitter-mounted guards. An overarm guard has an arm that extends over the table and supports the barrier (1–17). The splitter and anti-kickback pawls are secured under the throat plate (1–18). When crosscuts or non-through cuts are made, the splitter and anti-kickback pawls may be removed by lifting the throat plate and either removing the splitter or pushing it down out of the way.

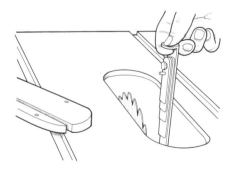

1–18. The splitter and anti-kickback pawls on this saw are secured under the table. They can be lifted up for use. Other saws have quick-disconnect fasteners for easy removal and replacement of the splitter and anti-kickback pawls. These are usually furnished with overarm guards.

Overarm guards work for most common cuts such as rip cuts, crosscuts, and miters as long as the workpiece does not interfere with the overarm support. They also work well for most non-through cuts. Overarm guards must also be removed when some resawing and tenoning operations are being performed. In such situations, the appropriate jigs, featherboards, and push sticks have to be used to control stock and keep hands clear of the blade.

MITER GAUGE

The miter gauge is a device used to crosscut wood or cut miters on the ends of stock. It slides in the slots milled into the table (1–19). The miter gauge guides the edges of stock into the blade. It has a tongue that fits into the table slot. The head controls the angle with its protractor-like movement. A clamping knob holds the angle setting at the desired position. Some miter gauges have stops that allow movement to a frequently used angle, such as 45 or 90 degrees.

In some cases, sandpaper facings are glued to the miter gauge to increase control over the work. Wooden jigs or backing boards are also attached to the miter gauge with screws or clamps (1–20).

1–19. The miter gauge slides in slots that have been milled into the table. The portion of the miter gauge that rests in the slot is known as the tongue.

1–20. Auxiliary faces are often attached to the miter gauge. These faces are usually held in place with wood screws. They increase control over the workpiece. Abrasives are sometimes glued to the faces to increase control.

These boards or jigs increase control over the workpieces and make the work safer and more accurate.

Also refer to Specialty Miter Gauge on page 31 for more information on miter gauges.

FENCE

The fence is a device used to control stock during rip cuts (cuts with the grain). The distance from the fence to the blade determines the width of the stock (1–21). The fence slides on a rail at the front of the saw table. It is clamped to the rail to hold the desired setting. On some table saws, there is a second rail on the outfeed end of the saw. In this case, the fence rides on both rails and

may clamp to the back rail, too. There is often a scale on the fence that can be adjusted to zero according to which blade is being used (1–22). Once it is adjusted to the blade in use, the scale will indicate the distance between the blade and fence. This will make ripping width easy to set.

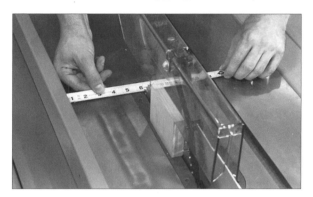

1–21. The fence is parallel to the blade and controls rip cuts. The rip dimension is equal to the distance between the blade and fence. The fence is locked to the rail or rails when a rip cut is being made. Many saws have a rip scale on the front rail to make fence adjustment fast and accurate.

1–22. This fence has a scale that indicates the distance between the blade and fence. The scale is adjusted for the blade being used.

THROAT PLATE

The throat plate, also known as a table or blade insert, covers the opening in the table that allows access to the blade arbor and the splitter-mounting bracket (1–23 and 1–24). The throat plate has a hole to allow clearance for the blade and splitter. It may be held in by gravity or there may be metal fasteners that hold it in place. The throat plate should sit even with the top of the table saw. Some throat plates are equipped with leveling screws for fine adjustment of the throat-plate lever with the tabletop (1–25).

Accessories

Accessories, or optional equipment, are not required for most table-saw operations, but for advanced operations this equipment can make work at the saw safer or more efficient. The most common optional equipment includes specialty miter gauges, tenoning jigs, featherboards, push sticks, anti-kickback devices, roller supports, power feeders, and rolling stands. Many of these accessories, such as the featherboards and push sticks, can be either bought or user-made.

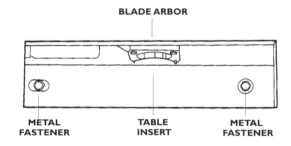

1–23. The throat plate is also known as the table insert. It is often held in place with screws. (Drawing courtesy of Sears Craftsman.)

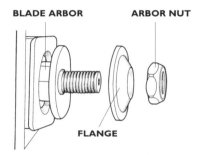

1–24. The blade arbor drives the blade. It is located beneath the throat plate. (Drawing courtesy of Sears Craftsman.)

1–25. The throat plate or table insert is removed to change blades. It may also be necessary to remove it when removing or replacing the splitter. This throat plate can be adjusted to table height; other throat plates cannot be adjusted. The throat plate must be in place for all operations.

ANTI-KICKBACK DEVICE

There are many types of anti-kickback devices marketed today. In most cases, they limit the travel of the work to a single path toward the blade. If the stock begins to travel toward the operator (kickback), these devices slow or stop the wood. They usually consist of wheels that turn in one direction only (the direction of feed). The wheels act as a brake in the event of a kickback (1–26). Anti-kickback devices can be used with the guard and splitter for through cutting. They can also be used independent of the guard for non-through cuts.

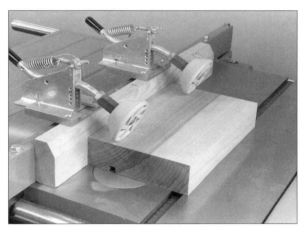

1–26. The wheels on this anti-kickback device turn only in the direction of stock feed. If the workpiece were to kick back, the wheels would slow or stop its velocity.

DUST-COLLECTION SYSTEM

For a clean shop and a healthier environment, a dust-collection system should be attached to the table saw. A dust-collection system gathers the dust and chips produced by the saw. In most cases, a hose of three to six inches in diameter transports the chips from the table saw to the dust collector. There are devices on the saw that funnel the chips toward the hose. The vacuum

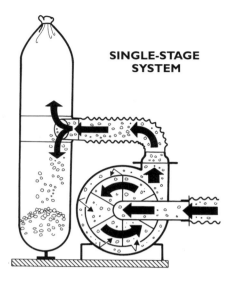

SINGLE-STAGE SYSTEM

1–27. This single-stage dust collector pulls all chips through the impeller. (Drawing courtesy of Delta International Machinery Corporation.)

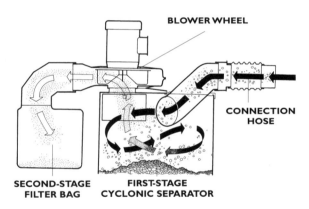

BLOWER WHEEL

CONNECTION HOSE

SECOND-STAGE FILTER BAG

FIRST-STAGE CYCLONIC SEPARATOR

1–28. This two-stage dust collector pulls only fine dust through the impeller. (Drawing courtesy of Delta International Machinery Corporation.)

from the dust collector moves the chips into the collector for later disposal.

A dust collector consists of an impeller or fan that generates air movement. On a single-stage dust collector (1–27), the chips and dust travel through the impeller. On a two-stage dust collector (1–28), the chips drop in a container in front of the impeller. Only the fine dust travels through the impeller into a dust bag. The two-stage dust collector separates large chips and metal parts (such as the arbor nut or washer) from the impeller. This reduces the likelihood of damage to the impeller or possible fire caused by sparking.

Dust collectors are rated by their horsepower and number of cubic feet per minute (CFM) of air they can move. The typical range of CFMs is about 300 to 1,000; this depends on the size and horsepower of the dust collector. The volume of chips generated determines the minimum CFM requirement. A typical table saw with a dedicated system (a system hooked up only to the table saw, and not also to other tools) would need about 300 CFMs.

Dust collectors make the air cleaner to breathe and reduce fire and explosive hazards. Sawdust can explode in the same way as grain dust will, and it should be treated as a hazard. Many of the treated woods and particleboard increase the hazard of breathing sawdust. Their additional chemicals are likely to be more hazardous than actual wood dust. Research has shown that wood dust has contributed to nasal cancer and upper respiratory problems in woodworkers.

The means by which dust-collection equipment is attached to the table saw varies from one model to the next. Most of the benchtop saws that would be used on the job site or in a small shop may have a dust port cut into their base. This may be fitted for the standard vacuum hose instead of a standard dust-collection hose port. There are many types of adapters that will make the attachment easy (1–29). In some cases, though, duct tape will have to be used (1–30).

On models that do not have a dust port, one can be cut into the base using a hole saw. Most of the bases are plastic or sheet metal. Select the position of the hole carefully. It should not interfere with the operation of the saw. It should also

1–29. Many adapters are available today that allow table-saw operators to use standard dust-collection hoses or shop vacuums to collect the dust. Plumbing fixtures are often used to adapt fittings.

1–30. This dust port has been adapted to field conditions with duct tape and a wire clamp. Many dust-collection setups require some form of adaptation.

be positioned to take advantage of the centrifugal force of the blade. *Benchtop* table saws have an open bottom, so a piece of plywood must be attached to the bottom to seal the container. If the saw is not placed on a flat surface, the dust collector may tear through the plywood bottom. How the saw is positioned for the work will determine the best way to collect the chips.

Contractor table saws are the most difficult to work with when collecting dust. This is because the stand is open under and at the back of the saw. Enclosing the stand is not that easy. The bottom can be enclosed using a piece of sheet

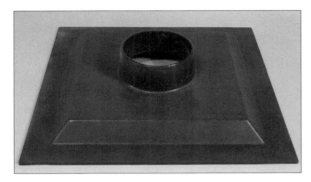

1–31. *This type of adapter can be used to enclose the opening under the blade on a contractor's saw. It can be held in place with sheet-metal screws.*

stock; in fact, this would be a good place to put a four-inch dust port (1–31). The problem is that the back cannot be enclosed, because if the blade is tilted, the motor also has to tilt. If the back is enclosed, then the motor cannot tilt. Some woodworkers have put a piece of cardboard on the back with an allowance for the belts when the saw is perpendicular to the table. This increases the pulling strength of the dust collector and deflects chips that are thrown by the blade. If the blade is tilted, then the cardboard must be removed. Cardboard is a good choice of material in case the operator forgets to remove it when the blade is tilted.

Cabinet saws are much easier to fit for dust collection. In most cases, the side where the motor tilts is open to allow for the arc of the motor. Most manufacturers offer a motor cover as an accessory. Another option is to build a box out of sheet stock. When building a box, hinge the door. It makes it easier to retrieve the arbor nut or washer if they are dropped. Retrofitting older models with a dust-collection system is not as easy as it is to set up a new model for dust collection. This is because the older models only offer a floor port. This port collects only the chips that drop to the floor. The newer models have a baffle, or shroud, that will direct the chips toward the dust-collection port. These models are more efficient than the older models. With time and ingenuity, ports and shrouds can be adapted to older models. Be certain that any device made does not interfere with the operation of the saw or cause chips to accumulate on the elevating-and-tilting mechanism(s).

One other consideration that should be factored into the setup of dust collection is easy removal and replacement of the collection hoses. This will make it easier to move from one saw to another. As discussed above, quick-disconnect devices can be clamped to the hoses that will make it easy to remove and replace the hose. An extension hose can also be used if an extra-long hose is required. This standardization of fittings reduces the number of adapters and the amount of tape that will have to be used.

With any dust-collection system, some provision has to be made for static electricity. The hazards of static electricity are first sparking, and second, shock. The sparking can be the source of ignition. This could ignite a slow-building fire that could destroy property and put life at risk. If the collection system is made of non-conducting materials, then a copper wire must run through the system to ground it from static electricity. Electric shock is not enough to injure the table-saw operator, yet it could cause him or her to react in such a manner that leads to contact with a saw blade or other hazard in the shop.

Another dust-collection consideration would be the fine dust that is not usually collected by the typical dust collector. Today there are dust filters that can be used in the field (1–32) or in the shop (1–33). These filtering systems remove the fine particles that hang in the air and would most likely be inhaled.

1–32. *This portable air-filtration system can reduce the amount of dust in the air dramatically. However, it should not be a substitute for a dust collector. (Photo courtesy of Sears Craftsman.)*

1–33. *This shop air-filtration system will improve air quality in any shop. It filters even the finest dust from the air particles so small they would be missed by the dust collector. (Photo courtesy of Sears Craftsman.)*

FEATHERBOARD

A featherboard is a commercial or user-made accessory that holds stock against the fence or table near the blade and keeps hands away from the cutting area (1–34). They are held in place by magnetic or clamping force. Featherboards can also be used as guards. They act as a barrier and can slow the velocity of a piece should it kick back.

Featherboards should never be used adjacent to the blade when a through cut is made. The spring action can cause binding in the saw cut and set up a kickback condition.

Making a Featherboard

A featherboard is an easy accessory to make. Use a piece of hardwood about ¾ inch thick, 3 to 4 inches wide, and 12 to 18 inches long. Make sure that it will be long enough to be clamped to the fence or table. Cut the end of the piece at an

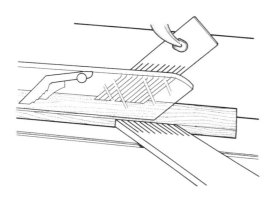

1–34. *These featherboards increase control over the stock by holding it against the fence and table.*

angle of 30 to 60 degrees using the miter gauge. (Refer to Miter Cuts on pages 83 to 89 for more information on cutting miters.) The angle is determined by how and where the featherboard will be attached (1–35 to 1–37). Mark the feather length on the work. Longer feathers are more springy.

Select a piece of stock approximately ³⁄₁₆ to ¼ inch thick to use as a spacer. Set the dis-

tance between the blade and fence using the spacer (1–38). Make sure that the blade is about ⅛ inch higher than the stock thickness. Position the stock against the auxiliary fence and make a cut to the layout line (1–39). Shut off the saw and allow the blade to come to a complete stop before releasing the stock. Leave the stock in place. Reposition the fence using a second spacer.

MAKING A FEATHERBOARD

1–35. Making a featherboard. The first step is to decide where to clamp it and then to mark the angle on the board.

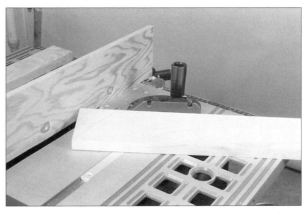

1–36. The miter gauge is set to copy the angle marked on the work. Secure the miter head at the angle by clamping the clamp knob.

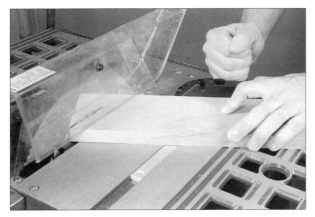

1–37. Next, the face miter cut is made on the end of the workpiece. Refer to pages 83 to 84 for information on cutting face miters.

1–38. The first spacer is used to set the distance from the blade to the auxiliary fence. The fence is locked to the table.

(continued on following page)

MAKING A FEATHERBOARD (CONTINUED)

1–39. Making the first feather cut. Stop at the layout line, turn off the saw, and let the blade come to a complete stop.

1–40. With the work in the same position, loosen the fence and move it until the second spacer fits between the work and the auxiliary fence.

1–41. The process is repeated with the larger spacer until the featherboard is completed.

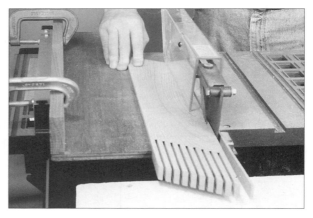

1–42. If the last feather is too small, it can be sawn completely off.

The second spacer is as thick as the feather and the saw kerf or about ⅛ inch thicker than the first spacer. Use it to space the fence to the edge of the work (1–40). Lock the fence and then release the work from the anti-kickback pawls if necessary. Turn on the saw and make the second cut. Stop at the layout line, shut off the saw, and hold the stock until the blade comes to a complete stop. Release the fence and insert the larger spacer. Lock the fence and repeat the process. Continue this process until the featherboard is complete (1–41). If the last feather is wider or narrower than the others, continue the last cut to trim the featherboard so that the feathers are uniform in width (1–42). The featherboard is now ready for use.

POWER FEEDER

A power feeder is a motorized feed unit equipped with an endless belt or three or more wheels (1–43). When the power feeder is in its operating position, its metal base is bolted to the outfeed edge of the saw to the left of the blade. A column is positioned in the base. A metal casting on the column supports another metal column, which is parallel to the tabletop. On the end of

1–43. The power feeder uses urethane wheels to guide stock through the blade. It is commonly used for rip cuts. The base behind the motor is actually bolted to the saw's extension wing.

1–44. The wheels drive the wood into the blade. The last wheel will push the work and cutoff past the blade for easy retrieval.

the column is the drive motor with wheels or an endless belt to push stock through the blade.

The power feeder can be adjusted on all faces and is capable of holding stock against the fence or table for feeding purposes (1–44). Power feeders keep the operator farther from the blade and reduce fatigue and the likelihood of a kickback.

PUSH STICK

A push stick is a wooden (1–45) or plastic (1–46) commercial or user-made device that guides stock through the blade. It keeps fingers away from the blade and provides greater control over the work. A push stick is essential when a narrow rip cut is being made.

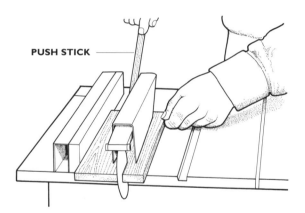

PUSH STICK

1–45. A push stick is used to guide and control stock as it passes through the blade. It keeps hands farther from the blade and allows greater control over the work.

Push sticks have many different sizes and shapes. The wooden ones are usually user-made. They are cut out on the band saw, scroll saw, or portable saber saw. Plywood and other sheet-stock scrap make good push sticks. Be sure to smooth and round all edges before using the push stick. This will make the push stick more comfortable and prevent sharp edges from splitting the skin if they are forced into the hand by

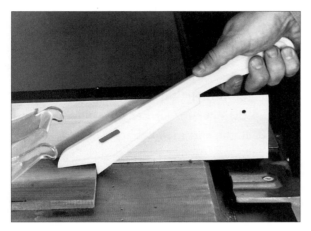

1–46. This commercial push stick is made of molding plastic. It is comfortable in the hand and adds distance between the operator's hands and the point of operation.

a kickback. Use the patterns shown in 1–47 and 1–48 to make a push stick for the table saw. Keep a few extra push sticks near the saw.

Push sticks are usually made from scraps of ½- or ¾-inch plywood. To make one, lay out the pattern and cut it on a band saw. Sand the handle area and round the edges, for comfort and safety. A sharp corner could cut you in the event of a kickback.

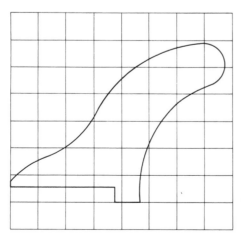

1–47. This push-stick pattern is on a grid made of one-inch squares. Make a few push sticks from this pattern to keep by the table saw.

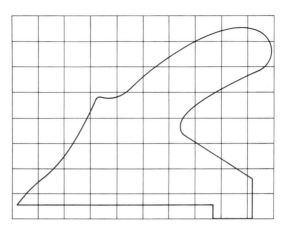

1–48. This push-stick pattern is also on a grid made of one-inch squares. It provides greater control over stock being ripped.

ROLLER SUPPORTS

When long pieces of stock have to be ripped, the table is too short to support the piece. When this occurs, a roller support or series of roller supports are used to support the work. The roller support should be set at the same height as the saw table or slightly lower (¼ to ½ inch lower). The stand should be perpendicular to the path of the workpiece (1–49). When the rollers are not perpendicular to the path of the workpiece, the roller support tends to pull the workpiece off the intended path. This can result in a kickback, stock burning, or stock of incorrect dimensions.

1–49. A roller support prevents the workpiece from lifting off the blade. Make sure that the roller support is perpendicular to the blade and well balanced.

SPECIALTY MITER GAUGE

A specialty miter gauge has features such as stop rods to control length and clamping mechanisms to hold stock securely while the cut is being made (1–50). There are many types of specialty miter gauge. One type can be set up to cut both miter cuts with one setting (1–51 and 1–52). These complementary cuts ensure tight-fitting miter joints. There are also specialty miter gauges for cutting box joints. These miter gauges have fine adjustments to perfect box-joint spacing.

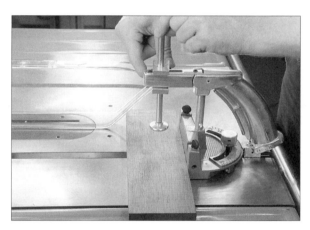

1–50. This miter gauge has a built-in clamping device. The clamp rod holds stock securely against the tongue of the miter gauge.

TENONING JIG

The tenoning jig is a helpful accessory to use when the end grain of a board must be positioned on the table. It holds stock securely while the end is machined. Tenoning jigs ride in the miter slot (1–53). Their clamping system makes it easy to control large pieces of stock. Some tenoning jigs allow the stock to be positioned at an angle for specialty cuts.

Refer to Through Mortises on pages 61 and 62 for information on using tenoning jigs to cut through mortises.

MITER CUTS WITH A SPECIALTY MITER GAUGE

1–51. The left miter is cut using a specialty miter gauge.

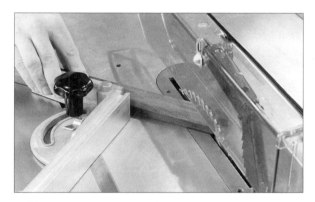

1–52. When the auxiliary face is moved about two inches, the right miter can be cut using the same setup.

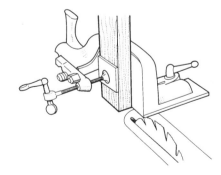

1–53. The tenoning jig rides in the miter-gauge slot and holds stock vertically when joinery is being cut. The paths of some tenoning jigs are controlled by the fence.

Maximizing Table-Saw Performance

Sometimes a table saw will not be performing up to its capabilities. Indications of this are that the table saw is not producing good-quality cuts or that tear-out, burning, or creeping (the tendency of the board to creep along the face of the miter gauge during crosscuts) is occurring. There are three main reasons for this: too fine a blade is being used, the saw is misaligned, or the saw is vibrating. The information below describes how to determine which condition is affecting table-saw performance, and lists procedures for eliminating this condition. In addition, refer to Troubleshooting Guidelines on pages 35 and 36 to deal with specific cutting problems.

IMPROPER BLADE USAGE

The best way to determine the cause of a poorly cutting table saw is to change blades. This is because most woodworkers use too fine a blade for most operations, and it results in slower feed speeds, which generate heat and burning.

If burning is occurring, put a coarse blade on the saw. If burning still occurs, then there is probable an alignment problem with the blade, splitter, or fence.

MISALIGNED TABLE SAW

Alignment problems occur because the saw was handled roughly or was moved around with the fence rails used as handlebars. Indications that a table saw is misaligned are stock tear-out, burning, or creeping, depending on the type of cut being made. If a crosscut is being made, the two most common problems are tear-out and creeping. If tear-out is occurring on the top surface of the board when the teeth at the back of the blade enter the saw kerf, it

FINE AND COARSE BLADES

The information in this and in subsequent chapters often refers to fine and coarse blades. Fine blades have smaller teeth than coarse blades. They are designed for more delicate work. Coarse blades are blades with large teeth, and are designed for heavy or fast work. A fine 10-inch blade would be one with 60 or more teeth. A medium-pitch 10-inch blade would be one with 40 to 60 teeth. A coarse 10-inch blade has 24 to 40 teeth.

means that the back teeth are not following the front teeth. The back teeth will cause burning and tear-out on the side of the kerf they are nearer to. If the board is creeping, the direction it creeps indicates which way the back teeth are misaligned.

Before checking for alignment, be sure to disconnect the saw from its power source. The first thing to check for is that the blade and miter-gauge slot are properly aligned. *Always check this first.* This requires measurement from the miter-gauge slot. Raise the blade to full height and select a tooth that points toward the slot. Measure the distance from the slot to the selected tooth at the back of the table (1–54). Now rotate the blade until the selected tooth is at the front of the saw and make the same measurement (1–55). If the measurements are not equal, the saw must be realigned.

Some saws can be aligned from the top of the table. Others require that the adjustments be made from the underside of the table. This is typical of a contractor saw. Cabinet saws can be adjusted the easiest. The four bolts that hold the table to the top of the cabinet are loosened and the table is turned slightly.

If a coarse blade is being used to rip stock and burning occurs, this could indicate misalignment of the blade, splitter, or fence. If the blade is properly aligned with the miter-gauge slot, then either the fence or splitter is misaligned. To check the fence's alignment, move it to the miter-gauge slot and lock it to the table. The fence should be parallel to the miter-gauge slot. If it is not, it must be adjusted. In most cases, there is one (sometimes two) bolt(s) on top of the fence that can be loosened for alignment purposes (1–56). If the fence locks to the back and front of the table, then the rear clamping mechanism must be loosened to align the fence. This mechanism is usually above the lock or clamp

CHECKING ALIGNMENT

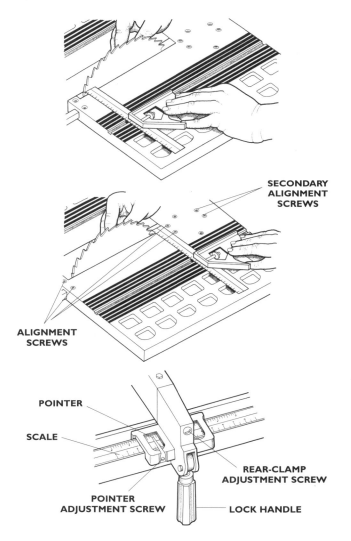

I–54. *Checking the alignment of a saw blade first consists of measuring the distance from the miter-gauge slot to a select tooth on the blade at the front of the table. (Drawing courtesy of Skil Power Tools.)*

SECONDARY ALIGNMENT SCREWS

I–55. *Then the distance from the miter-gauge slot to a selected tooth at the back of the table is measured. If the saw blade is in alignment, both distances will be equal. (Drawing courtesy of Skil Power Tools.)*

ALIGNMENT SCREWS

POINTER

SCALE

REAR-CLAMP ADJUSTMENT SCREW

POINTER ADJUSTMENT SCREW

LOCK HANDLE

I–56. *Both the bolt on top of the fence and the rear-clamp adjustment screw must be loosened so that the fence can be aligned. (Drawing courtesy of Skil Power Tools.)*

(continued on following page)

CHECKING ALIGNMENT (CONTINUED)

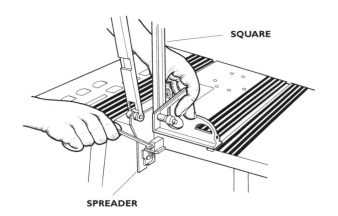

1–57. To ensure proper alignment, the splitter should be centered in the saw kerf. This will prevent the saw from binding. (Drawing courtesy of Skil Power Tools.)

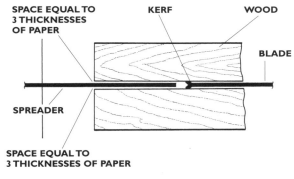

LOOKING DOWN ON SAW

1–58. The splitter should be square to the table when the blade is square to the table. This ensures that the splitter will be in the middle of the kerf at any angular setting of the blade. (Drawing courtesy of Skil Power Tools.)

---

handle. Be sure to tighten it after making the adjustment.

If neither the blade nor the fence is misaligned, the problem is most likely the splitter. The splitter is thinner than the blade, so it should be centered on the blade (1–57). It should be perpendicular to the table when the blade is perpendicular to the table (1–58). This ensures that

it will remain parallel to the blade when the blade is tilted.

Alignment procedures may vary from one saw to another. Always check the owner's manual for adjustment specifics. Check the saw's alignment periodically. A misaligned saw can contribute to kickback.

SETTING UP A TABLE SAW

Setting up a table saw properly is the key to minimizing vibration, described on the following pages.

Follow these procedures:

1. Make sure all four legs of the saw touch the floor. Shim them if necessary.
2. Bolt the saw securely to the stand.
3. Make sure the pulleys are in perfect alignment so that the belt does not generate vibration.
4. Make sure the pulleys run true on their shafts. Replace them if necessary.
5. Make sure the blade fits the saw arbor snugly.
6. Tighten the arbor nut properly.
7. Make sure the arbor washer is smooth and bears evenly against the blade.
8. Make sure all blade adjustments have been locked/tightened before sawing.

MINIMIZING VIBRATION

A table saw that vibrates excessively can affect the quality of the cut. Reducing vibration pays dividends in work quality. The best way to ensure that the table saw does not vibrate excessively is to set it up properly. Setting Up a Table Saw on page 34 describes the procedures for setting up the table saw correctly.

Inexpensive blades can also cause vibration.

The vibration from an inexpensive blade can be reduced by adding saw collars on a dampener. These accessories pull the blade into a truer orbit. They can also move the position of the blade on the arbor. Be sure to readjust the splitter and check for blade clearance in the throat plate after installation.

If excessive vibration still occurs after the table saw is set up correctly and a dampener or collars are added, consult the owner's manual.

TROUBLESHOOTING GUIDELINES

The information in this section will enable the reader to identify the reason for a specific cutting problem and provides methods for resolving it.

Problem	Reason	Remedy
Saw will not start	Power cord not plugged in	Plug cord in
	Fuse or circuit breaker tripped	Replace fuse or reset tripped circuit breaker
	Cord damaged	Have cord replaced by an authorized service center or service station
	Burned-out switch	Have switch replaced by an authorized service center or service station
Blade does not come up to speed	Extension cord too light or too long	Replace with adequate cord
	Low house voltage	Contact your electric company
Excessive vibration	Failure to tighten tilt-lock handle	Refer to saw manual
	Blade out of balance	Discard blade and use different blade
	Saw not mounted securely to stand or workbench	Tighten all mounting hardware
	Arbor nut not tight	Refer to saw manual
Cannot make square cut when crosscutting	Miter gauge not adjusted properly	Refer to saw manual
Cut binds, burns, or stalls motor when ripping	Dull blade with improper tooth set	Sharpen or replace blade
	Warped board	Make sure concave or hollow side is facing down and feed it slowly
	Rip fence not parallel to blade	Refer to saw manual
	Splitter out of alignment	Refer to saw manual
	Feed rate too slow	Slow down feed rate
	Dull blade	See sharpening service
	Pitch buildup on teeth	Use pitch remover

(continued on following page)

TROUBLESHOOTING GUIDELINES (*CONTINUED*)

The information in this section will enable the reader to identify the reason for a specific cutting problem and provides methods for resolving it.

Problem	Reason	Remedy
Cut not true at 90- or 45-degree positions	Alignment screws not adjusted properly	Refer to saw manual
Tilt-lock handle of elevation wheel hard to move	Blade tilt-lock handle does not loosen when making tilt adjustment	Refer to saw manual
	Sawdust on depth-screw threads	Refer to saw manual
Wavy cut	Fence not parallel to blade Dull blade Splitter not aligned with blade	Reset fence See sharpening service Check setup
Stock climbs over blade	Dull blade Feed rate too fast	See sharpening service Slow down feed rate
Workpiece difficult to feed	Fence not parallel to blade Feed rate too fast Dull Blade Pitch buildup on teeth	Reset fence Slow down feed rate See sharpening service Use pitch remover
Blade wobbles or deflects	Blade too low Blade too thin Dull blade Feed rate too fast Bearings worn Fence not parallel to blade	Raise teeth above stock Use stiffening collars See sharpening service Slow down feed rate Refer to saw manual Consult saw manual to reset fence
Excessive noise	Blade vibration Dull blade	Use stiffening collars See sharpening service

Blade-Selection Factors

If the proper blade is not used for a specific cutting application, the result will be a poor-quality cut. When determining which blade to use, the table-saw operator has to consider the material being cut, the desired finish, and the type of cut being made. Then he or she has to determine which blade has the cutting characteristics to produce a high-quality cut in this situation (2–1). Such a determination can only be made if the operator has a knowledge of the blade as relates to three areas: whether the blade is tool-steel or carbide-tipped; the type of teeth it has, and their configuration; and the specific function for which it was designed. This information is given below. Also refer to Chapter 4 for a discussion of blades used to cut wood and non-wood material.

TOOL-STEEL AND CARBIDE-TIPPED BLADES

There are two general types of blade: tool-steel and carbide-tipped. They each have clearance on both sides of the blade. The clearance prevents the plate from dragging in the kerf (cut made by the blade). Clearance in tool-steel blades is accomplished by the blade's tooth set. Tooth set is an offset or bend in the teeth (2–2). The set alternates from one side to the other around the blade.

Carbide-tipped blades have small pieces of carbide brazed to a tool-steel plate (2–3). These blades have a clearance ground onto the sides of the carbide tips. There are differences in the cutting performances of tool-steel and carbide-tipped blades. Tool-steel blades do not usually produce as high quality a cut as carbide-tipped blades. They also do not stay sharp nearly as long. They are not appropriate for materials such as particleboard and fiber-core plywood. However, they do not generate as much friction as carbide-tipped blades. Increased friction can potentially overwork the motor and cause burning on both edges of the saw kerf. This will ruin the appearance of the cut and reduce edge-gluing strength. Therefore, tool-steel blades may be more suitable in certain situations such as cutting thick material when reducing friction will improve the cut. For example, a heavy cut on a light-duty saw can be accomplished with a coarse tool-steel blade. For all other cuts, carbide-tipped blades are best.

Some carbide-tipped blades have a chip-limiting feature that slows the feed speed because it limits the size of the bite any tooth can take (2–4). This also reduces the chance of kickback because each tooth has such a small grip on the wood. The blade's plate and rim prevent the stock from feeding too quickly into the blade. Chip-limiting blades are ideal for beginning woodworkers.

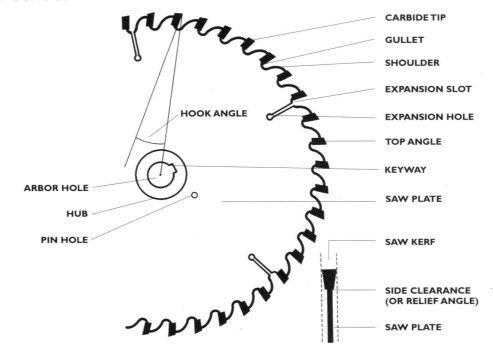

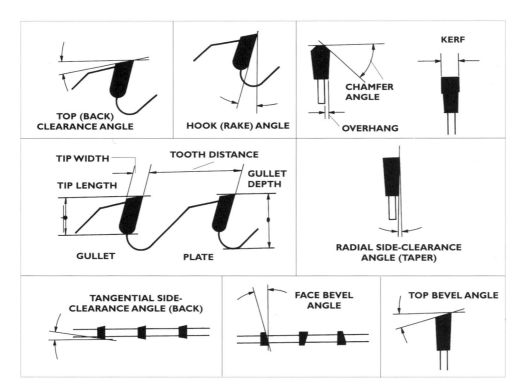

2–1. This drawing highlights the parts of a table-saw blade and clarifies the terminology used to describe them. (Drawing courtesy of Nordic Saw and Tool Manufacturing.)

2–2. Tool-steel blades have a bend or set in each of their teeth. Each tooth is bent in the opposite direction as the one before or after it. The set gives the body of the blade clearance in the saw kerf. Too little clearance can cause binding and kickback.

2–3. The carbide tips are brazed into a seat that has been cut into the blade's plate. The carbide tips are wider than the plate. This gives the blade clearance in the saw cut or kerf.

2–4. A chip-limiting blade slows feed speed and reduces the chance of a kickback.

TOOTH STYLE AND CONFIGURATION

There are four basic tooth configurations used on carbide-tipped blades: alternate top bevel, alternate top bevel and raker, triple chip, and flat top (2–5). The tooth configuration of the blade will indicate which job it is best suited for.

Alternate-top-bevel teeth are designed primarily for *crosscutting*, although they are also used for ripping. When they are used for ripping, feed speed is less than ideal. Alternate-top-bevel teeth come to a point on alternate sides of the blade. The points cut the edges of the kerf before the middle of the kerf is cut out. This reduces the chance of tear-out.

A blade with alternate-top-bevel-and-raker teeth is ideal for *ripping* and *crosscutting*. The alternate top-bevel teeth ensure good results when crosscutting, and the raker tooth cleans out the kerf during rip cuts.

Blades with a triple-chip tooth configuration are designed to cut *plywood, particleboard, melamine board, and other wood-based sheet stock.* (Refer to Chapter 4 for more information on cutting these materials.) One tooth is a flat-top tooth, and the next tooth looks like a flat-top tooth with the corners cut off. The tooth with the corners cut off separates the kerf, and the flat-top tooth planes the sides for a smooth, tear-out-free cut.

Blades with a triple-chip tooth configuration are also used to cut solid stock, but generally they are not as efficient as blades with alternate-top-bevel or alternate-top-bevel-and-raker teeth.

Blades with flat-top teeth should be used for one function: ripping. Since wood fibers go the long way in a board, the flat-top tooth will rip the wood smoothly. The quality of the cut diminishes greatly when a blade with flat-top teeth is used for crosscutting.

Flat-Top Grind (FT). *Generally, for cutting material with grain. Large gullet accepts greater chip loads, permits higher feed rates. Excellent for ripping where speed of cut is more important than quality of cut. Teeth with square or flat-top shape act as chisels, cutting material with chisel-like action. Teeth also serve as rakers to clean out the cutting or chips.*

Triple-Chip- &-Flat Grind (TC & F). *Recommended for cutting brittle and/or hard abrasive materials. Two shapes of teeth—alternate triple-edge and flat-top—for dual-action cutting. Triple-edge teeth cut down center of kerf. Flat-top raker teeth follow to clean out material from both sides. TC & F blades with negative hook angles are also recommended for cutting non-ferrous metals. Negative hook angle prevents climbing; gives total control over feed rate.*

Alternate-Top-Bevel Grind (ATB). *For across-the-grain cutting and/or cut-off and trimming operations on undefined grain. Top bevel- shaped teeth sever the material with shearing action alternately left and right. The ATB blade with the higher number of teeth will produce the higher quality of finish cut. Where finish is no concern, select the blade with fewer teeth.*

Alternate Top Bevel & Raker (ATB & R). *Excellent for cutting operations with and/or across the grain. Achieves a fairly high level of quality over wide range of cuts. Two sets of shearing-action alternate left and right top bevel teeth,   followed by a raking-action flat-top tooth with large, round gullet to facilitate chip removal.*

2–5. *Common tooth designs used on carbide-tipped blades. Each tooth design is described under the illustration of the design. (Drawing courtesy of Delta International Machinery Corporation.)*

GENERAL-SAWING BLADES

Three blades will suffice for general sawing needs. For a 10-inch saw, select a rip blade with about 24 teeth (refer to 2–7). This will be coarse enough to handle any thickness the saw will accommodate.

The second blade should be a crosscut or cutoff blade with 40 teeth (2–8). This blade will handle most general cutoff work. A finer-cutting blade with 60 teeth will complete the selection. Use it to cut finished pieces to length.

BLADE-OVERVIEW CHART

Table-saw blades are designed for specific cutting applications. Use the information provided here to determine which blade is best suited for the task at hand:

Chisel-Tooth Combination Blade. A blade with a chisel-tooth blade edge specially designed for general-purpose ripping and crosscutting. Produces fast, smooth cuts. Can be used at maximum speed in most cutting applications.

Combination Blade. This blade is used for general-service ripping and crosscutting. It has the correct number of teeth to cut chips rather than scrape sawdust (2–6).

Crosscut Blade. This blade is designed specifically for fast, smooth crosscutting. Makes a smoother cut than the combination blade.

Flooring Blade. This blade should be used on jobs when occasional nails may be encountered. Especially useful in cutting through flooring.

Framing/Rip Combination Blade. A 40-tooth blade for fascia, roofing, siding, sub-flooring, and framing, and for making rip cuts, crosscuts, and cutting miters. Gives fast, smooth finishes when cutting with the grain of both soft and hard woods.

Friction Blade. This blade is ideal for cutting corrugated, galvanized sheets and sheet metal up to 16 gauge. Cuts faster, with less dirt, than an abrasive disc. Blade is taper-ground for clearance.

Metal-Cutting Blade. This blade has teeth shaped and set for cutting aluminum, copper, lead, and other soft metals.

Planer Blade. This blade makes both rip and crosscuts. Ideal for interior woodwork. Hollow ground to produce the finest-possible saw cut finish.

Plywood Blade. A hollow-ground, hard-chromed blade especially designed for exceptionally smooth cuts in plywood.

Rip Blade. This blade is designed to make rip cuts fast. Minimum binding and better chip clearance given by large teeth (2–7).

2–6. This 50-tooth combination blade is considered a general-duty blade for a 10-inch table saw. It has a chip-limiting feature and laser-cut slots to reduce noise. (Photo courtesy of CMT Tools.)

2–7. A rip blade with 24 teeth. Rip blades have larger teeth that provide for minimum binding and better chip clearance. (Photo courtesy of CMT Tools.)

2–8. A 48-tooth, carbide-tipped blade designed for crosscutting and trimming plastic laminates.

2–9. An 80-tooth blade designed to cut melamine-faced particleboard. (Photo courtesy of CMT Tools.) Refer to Chapter 4 for information on cutting particleboard and other sheet stock.

If you wish to compromise on the three blades described above, select a 50-tooth ATB-(alternate-top-bevel-)and-raker blade. It will do most jobs and produce satisfactory cuts in most materials.

2–10. An 80-tooth blade designed to cut miters in solid stock. Refer to Chapter 5 for information on cutting miters.

Select additional blades as needed. The blade should be determined by the material being cut, the desired finish, and the type of cut being made (2–9 and 2–10).

Blade-Selection Guidelines on the following page contains information to help make this decision.

Changing Blades

Saw blades should be changed when dull or when the blade does not fit the job. The procedure for changing blades is about the same for all table saws. Before beginning it, disconnect the saw from the power source. This may require unplugging the saw or shutting off a circuit. Always test the power switch to be sure that the power is off. Remember, when changing blades or handling them in any matter to be careful. A sharp (or dull) blade can cut you.

The first step is to remove the throat plate. Raise or remove the guard to gain access to it. The throat plate may be held in with fasteners or by gravity. Use the saw's wrench or wrenches to

BLADE-SELECTION GUIDELINES

The following guidelines will help the table-saw operator determine which blade to use in different cutting situations:

❶ Use blades with larger teeth to make rip cuts. Use a rip blade when only rip cuts are being made.

❷ Fine blades–blades with smaller teeth–produce a smoother cut but need a slower feed rate, so use the *coarsest* blade that will produce satisfactory results. Illus. 2–11 shows how to accomplish this.

❸ Use blades with more set when cutting green lumber or construction lumber. This is due to the increased moisture content in the lumber.

❹ Use hollow-ground blades and paneling blades *only* for true, dry cabinet-grade lumber. They have less side clearance and could burn in rougher and thicker pieces of stock. Also, remove any specialty or high-quality blades as soon as the job is done.

❺ Use a smaller-diameter blade if the saw being used has less than 1½ horsepower. For example, if it is a 10-inch table saw, an 8-inch blade should be used. The smaller blade requires less energy to turn, so there is more energy left to cut wood. The peripheral speed of the blade (rim speed) decreases, so the stock should be fed a little more slowly. A coarser blade should be used to compensate for the slower feed speed. Also, smaller-diameter blades reduce blade deflection, in which the blade bounces away from the workpiece. Smaller blades will not cut as deeply, but most woodworkers rarely need to use the full depth of the blade. In those cases when it is needed, use a larger-diameter blade.

No matter what size or type of blade, three teeth should be in the workpiece at all times.

❻ Never use a dull blade. A dull blade may lose side clearance. This can cause burning as the cut is made. A dull blade is unsafe and can cause a kickback. (Refer to Sharpening Dull Blades on pages 46 and 47 for information on sharpening blades.)

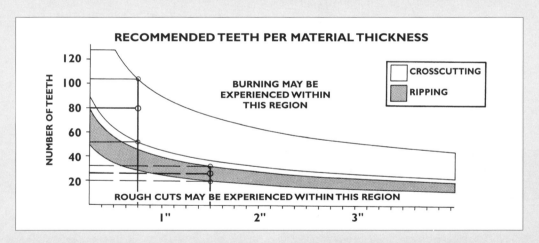

RECOMMENDED TEETH PER MATERIAL THICKNESS

BURNING MAY BE EXPERIENCED WITHIN THIS REGION

☐ CROSSCUTTING
▨ RIPPING

NUMBER OF TEETH

120 100 80 60 40 20

ROUGH CUTS MAY BE EXPERIENCED WITHIN THIS REGION

1"   2"   3"

2–11. A drawing and instructions that will help the table-saw operator determine the number of teeth a blade should have for a specific job. This consists of doing the following: 1. Use the bottom scale to find the material thickness that will be cut. 2. Extend a vertical line up into the shaded area that matches the cut being made (rip or crosscut). 3. Extend a horizontal line from the point where the vertical line enters the shaded area and a line from where it exits. These two lines represent the maximum and minimum number of teeth that should be used to make the cut. 4. Extend a horizontal line that is centered between the first two horizontal lines. The line represents the ideal number of teeth that should be used to make the cut. (Chart courtesy of Freud.)

CHANGING BLADES

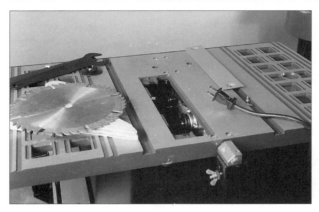

2–12. *The new blade ready to be mounted to the arbor. The power has been disconnected, the throat plate has been removed, and the arbor washer and arbor nut are handy.*

2–13. *Mount the blade on the arbor. The fit should be snug, and the plate should bear evenly against the inner arbor washer.*

2–14. *Both wrenches are being used to tighten the arbor nut. Do not over-tighten it.*

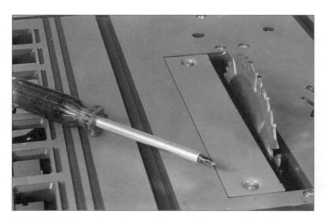

2–15. *Replace the throat plate and secure the fasteners. Make sure that the blade plate does not contact the throat plate.*

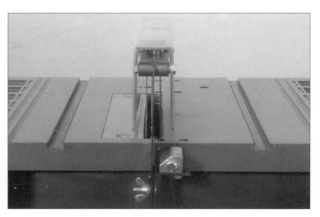

2–16. *When the guard is replaced, the splitter should line up with the blade. Make any needed adjustments.*

remove the arbor nut. Some motor-driven saws have left-hand threads, while most motorized saws may have either right- or left-hand threads. If the saw has only one wrench, a push stick or scrap may have to be used to hold the blade while the arbor nut is being loosened. The blade that has been removed should be stored away, and a new blade selected for use (2–12).

Next, the new blade should be mounted on the arbor. Make sure it is seated against the inside arbor washer (2–13). Check to see that the size of the arbor hole and size of the arbor match. The blade should fit snugly on the arbor. Replace the outer arbor washer and arbor nut.

Use the wrench or wrenches to tighten the arbor nut (2–14). Do not overtighten the arbor nut. If only one wrench is being used, the blade should be held between the thumb and index finger. Use the other hand to tighten the arbor nut. When the blade can no longer be held, the arbor nut is tight enough.

Next, the throat plate is replaced and secured in position (2–15). Turn the blade over by hand to be sure that it does not contact the throat plate. Reposition or mount the guard; check to be sure that it is aligned with the splitter (2–16). Now, power can be restored and the sawing begun.

Blade-Maintenance Techniques

PROTECTING BLADES

Blades should be protected from damage when not in use. The teeth of blades in storage should not touch (2–17). Such contact can dull or break carbide teeth, and will dull steel blades. Hang blades individually or with spacers between them. This will keep them sharp. Protect blades from corrosion. Corrosion will deteriorate a

2–17. *When blades are stored, their teeth should not touch. Contact with other blades can dull the teeth.*

sharp cutting edge. To protect the blades, add a light coat of oil or wax. Remember, Teflon-coated blades do not rust.

Never lay a blade on the cast-iron surface of the table saw. The set of the teeth causes them to scratch the table and become dull. Lay the blade on a scrap of stock when changing blades (refer to 2–12).

REMOVING PITCH

When a circular-saw blade becomes hot, pitch will accumulate on it. Pitch (wood resin) is a brown, sticky substance that looks like varnish. As pitch accumulates on the blade, it acts as an insulator. This keeps the blade from dissipating heat and causes it to become dull faster.

Pitch, which appears either on the blade itself or on the carbide tips, is usually an indication that the blade being used has too little set for the job. It can also mean that the blade is too dull to cut or that it is misaligned. In some cases, the blade accumulates pitch and smokes when it is installed backwards (teeth pointing the wrong way). Some blades are Teflon-coated to resist pitch accumulation, but the Teflon wears off after two or three resharpenings. Blades with newer Teflon coatings resist wear better.

Commercial pitch removers can be used to clean blades. Liquid cleansers like Fantastic and Top Job, as well as oven cleaners, work well (2–18). Avoid using abrasives to remove pitch. Abrasives leave scratches that make it easier for pitch to anchor itself to the blade

2–18. Oven cleaner is one of the most effective blade cleaners/pitch removers available. Some oven cleaners are caustic; be sure to follow the manufacturer's instructions.

SHARPENING DULL BLADES

Some indications of a dull blade include:
1. The stock tends to climb over the blade.
2. The blade smokes or gives off a burnt odor.
3. Increased effort is needed to feed the stock into the blade.
4. The saw no longer cuts a straight line.

Dull blades can also be identified by visual inspection. Look at the teeth. The teeth on blades used for rip cuts should come to an edge (2–19). The edge should be a straight line and not rounded. The teeth on blades used for crosscutting should come to a point (2–20). The two cutting angles should form a straight line to the point of the tooth.

Also check the blade for broken carbide tips. Replace broken tips when resharpening. (Only a qualified resharpening service should do this.)

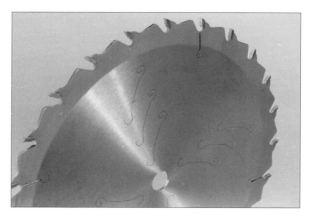

2–19. The rip teeth on this carbide-tipped blade come to an edge. There is no evidence of rounding.

2–20. The tool-steel teeth on this blade come to an edge. When flat spots replace the points, the blade is dull.

This is much more expensive than sharpening. Keep carbide blades sharp and broken tips will not be a problem.

Carbide teeth stay sharp longer than steel teeth, but they also become dull more quickly. If a dull carbide blade is left on the saw, the brittle teeth will crack or shatter. The sharpness of a carbide tip can be determined by dragging a fingernail across it. It should cut a chip (remove a curl from the fingernail). If it does not (if the fingernail slides across the tip), it is too dull to cut properly. Disconnect the saw to check a blade that is mounted.

In most cases, it is best to have blades sharpened by a professional sharpening service. Such services can be found in the Yellow Pages. The equipment they use is very accurate, but too expensive for the individual. Find a reliable service and develop a good working relationship.

When trying a new service, do not send them your best blades. Have them sharpen one or two general-duty blades first. Inspect the blades carefully. If the results are not satisfactory, try another sharpening service.

Make a board for transporting blades to the sharpening service or anywhere else. Put cardboard spacers between the blades (refer to 2–17). This will make the blades safer and easier to transport. It will also keep them well protected and sharp. Another approach is to buy a carrying case (2–21).

PREVENTING BROKEN BLADE TEETH OR BRAZED JOINTS

Carbide teeth can break or the brazed joint securing them to the plate may fail. In either case, the table-saw operator may find a piece of the blade flying at him. Most tooth breakage or brazing failure is a result of a sudden shock or lateral thrust (a slap to the side of the carbide tooth).

Carbide is a hard and brittle material. It is designed to resist wear caused by tough abrasive materials such as particleboard, fiber-core plywood, and plastic laminate. This also makes the

2–21. This carrying board will accommodate a dado head and some blades. It protects the blades during storage or transportation. (Photo courtesy of CMT Tools.)

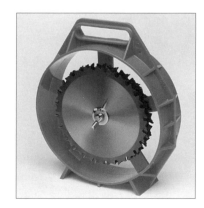

carbide tips susceptible to breakage during use. My first experience with this problem occurred when a student cleared cutoffs from the table with a push stick while the blade was running. When he accidentally contacted the side of the blade with the push stick, a carbide tip came flying off. The tip hit the fluorescent light twelve feet above. If there had been a guard on the saw and the operator had shut off the machine before clearing the scraps, this accident would not have happened! The guard is the first line of defense. Safety glasses are the second. Remember: The blade tips rotate at over 100 miles per hour!

Reasons for Broken Carbide Tips

Some common causes of tip breakage are:

I. Foreign objects or loose knots in the wood. Foreign objects such as a paneling nail or a drywall screw will usually break a few tips on the saw blade. This is because of the hardness of these materials. A loose common nail or knot will turn during the sawing process. As it turns, it produces enough stress on the hard, brittle carbide tip to cause it to fracture. And though a common nail that is not loose will usually not do any harm to the blade, it still should be removed from the wood before it is cut.

Inspect all stock before sawing it.

2. Rip cuts that are made on twisted stock. As the part twists through the blade, it is possible to generate enough side stress to fracture a carbide tip. It is best to cut twisted stock into shorter parts, where the twist is less pronounced.

3. Any play in the arbor or the arbor bearings.

4. A fence that pinches on the back side of the blade. This causes side stress and heat buildup at the carbide tips. Sufficient heat can soften a braze joint; that is why it is preferable to have carbide-tipped blades sharpened under a coolant.

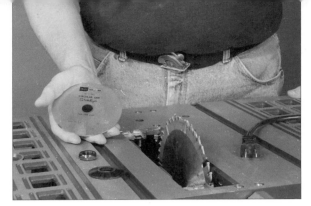

2–22. *Saw collars, or stabilizers, are mounted on either side of the saw blade to reduce vibration. They are like an oversized pair of arbor washers, so the concave side must face the blade.*

2–23. *Inspect the carbide tips of blades periodically for wear or damage. Always disconnect the power when making this check. Remember, even dull blades are sharp enough to cut.*

5. Operating the saw blade at a speed higher than specified on the blade. Many blades are designed for operation at 4,000 rpm or lower. If the blade is not designed for the saw speed, centrifugal force can actually break the brazed joint holding the tip to the plate.

6. Any freehand operation on the table saw. Always control the work with the fence or miter gauge during the cut.

7. Vibration. Use a dampener or saw collars to reduce blade vibration (2–22). Make sure that the saw is firmly seated on the floor so that it does not rock and cause vibration. When sawing thin stock, use a featherboard or other devices to ensure that the stock does not cause vibration while it is being cut. Refer to Minimizing Vibration on page 35 for more information.

8. Ripping thin strips without the use of a splitter. The fluttering of the thin strips can generate vibration and side stress.

9. Poor care and handling of saw blades. I have seen woodworkers pry the blade out of its protective case with a screwdriver, only to break a tip or two. Laying the blade on the cast-iron table while changing blades can also cause problems, because the saw-blade plate is actually being held off the table by the carbide tips. This can cause

lateral stress to the carbide tips or premature dulling. Contact between the saw blade and fence can also damage the blade and fence.

Reducing Tip Failure

Do the following to reduce tip failure:

1. Keep the saw blades clean. Pitch buildup can cause heat to build up at the tips, and it can also generate extra stress during the cut. Some forms of pitch are highly acidic and can actually break down the carbide at the cutting edge. This means that the tips are getting dull even when they are not being used!

2. Before mounting any carbide-tipped (or any other type of) blade on the saw, look it over carefully to be sure that it is in good condition (2–23). The brazed joints should look sturdy, and there should be no cracks in the carbide. Clean the tips if pitch buildup makes it impossible to inspect them. Be sure that the blade can handle the arbor speed. If not, do not use the blade; find one that can be used.

Broken carbide tips can be replaced by a competent sharpening service listed in the Yellow Pages, but the best policy is to do everything possible to eliminate the chance of tip breakage. If the sharpening service has to replace and grind more than three tips, it can cost 30 percent or more of the blade's actual cost.

Selecting a Dado Head

A dado head is used to cut dadoes and rabbets. Dadoes are U-shaped channels that go through a piece of stock (3–1). Rabbets are L-shaped channels that go along the edge of a piece of stock (3–2).

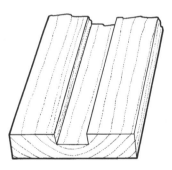

3–1. Dadoes, U-shaped channels that go through stock, can be cut with a dado head.

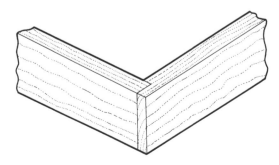

3–2. Rabbets, L-shaped channels that run along the stock's edge, can also be cut with a dado head.

There are actually three different types of dado head that can be used on the table saw: the stack dado head, the wobble dado head, and the adjustable V dado head. The *stack dado head* consists of two cutters, several chippers, and spacers (3–3). The chippers go between the cutters and increase the width of the dado cut. Two cutters cut a ¼-inch-wide dado; each chipper increases the dado width by ½, ⅛, or 1⁄16 inch. This type of dado head makes the best-quality cut, making the bottom of the dado square.

A *wobble dado head* consists of a large center hub and a saw blade (3–4). As the center hub turns, the blade inclines. When the dado head is mounted on the saw, the blade wobbles as it turns on the arbor. This causes it to cut a dado. The greater the incline of the blade, the wider the dado. Stack and wobble dado heads are sold widely.

The *twin-blade* or *adjustable V dado head* has a large center hub with two 8-inch-diameter, carbide-tipped cutters mounted on it (3–5). Each of these blades has 24 teeth. As the hub turns, the blades spread out at one end only. This makes it look like the letter V. In each revolution of the dado head, the saw blades remove all the stock in their paths, thus forming a dado. The adjustable V dado head is sold by DML and Sears. Sears calls its adjustable V dado head the Excalibur.

The adjustment collar at the center of the

COMPARING DADO HEADS

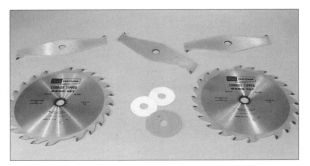

3–3. *A stack dado head consists of cutters (which look like saw blades), chippers (which go between the cutters to clean out the dado), and spacers (which space the dado to a precise width).*

3–4. *The wobble dado head has a large hub that keeps the blade rigid as it turns. The greater the incline of the blade, the wider the dado.*

3–5. *The adjustable V dado head has two carbide-tipped cutters. As the hub is turned, the blades form a V shape. The wider the V, the wider the dado.*

adjustable V dado head reveals the approximate dado width. The blade is marked at its widest point to simplify setup. It also has a depth-of-cut scale to help set dado depth.

The hubs on the adjustable V and the wobble dado heads are quite thick and may not fit on the arbor of some table saws. Make sure that the table saw will accommodate the dado head before buying it.

GUIDELINES FOR SELECTING AND USING DADO HEADS

❶ The quality of the cut varies from one brand of dado head to another, so before purchasing a dado head, ask other experienced woodworkers for their opinions.

❷ Whenever possible, purchase carbide-tipped dado heads. Avoid tool-steel dado heads; they will dull quickly.

❸ Special throat plates or inserts are used with all dado heads. The blade throat plate has too small an opening for the dado head. Never operate a table saw without the special throat plate in place.

❹ Proper alignment and cutting technique are as important as having a good-quality dado head. Even the best dado head will yield poor results on a table saw with an alignment problem. Similarly, a well-aligned saw with an inexpensive blade can yield acceptable results if light cuts are taken and the feed speed is not excessive.

Setting Up a Dado Head

Regardless of the type of dado head that is being used, the preliminary setup steps are the same. First, disconnect the saw from the power source. Put the electrical cord in plain view and try the switch to be sure it is "off" (3–6). Next, remove the throat plate. The throat plate may lift out or it may be secured in place with threaded fasten-

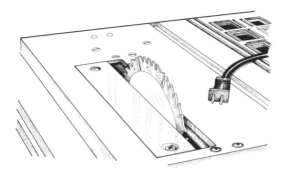

3–6. *To set up the dado head, disconnect the power and test the switch to be sure the power is disconnected. Lift or remove the guard to clear the throat plate or table insert.*

3–8. *Loosen the arbor nut with a wrench or pair of wrenches. When using only one wrench, a push stick may be used to hold the blade still.*

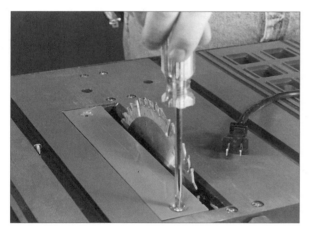

3–7. *Remove the throat plate to gain access to the arbor. This throat plate is held in place with screws.*

3–9. *Remove the arbor nut, arbor washer, and blade. Store the blade properly to keep it sharp and ready for the next job. Refer to page 45 for information on storing the blade properly.*

ers (3–7). Check your owner's manual to be sure.

The third step is to remove the blade. Inspect the threads to determine whether they are left-hand or right-hand threads. Use a wrench to loose the arbor nut (3–8). A push stick or a second wrench may be used to keep the blade from turning. Remove the nut, arbor washer, and blade (3–9). Store the blade so that it does not become dull or damaged.

The next steps in the setup of a dado head vary somewhat, depending on whether a stack dado or an adjustable dado is being mounted. Refer to the appropriate section below.

MOUNTING A STACK DADO HEAD

A stack dado head consists of cutters and chippers. The cutters (which look like saw blades) are always on the outside of the stock. They cut the two shoulders. The chippers are always mounted between two cutters; they remove the stock between the two shoulder cuts. When a ½-inch dado is desired, two cutters are used. For larger dadoes, a ¹⁄₁₆- or ⅛-inch chipper is positioned between the two cutters. Most stack dado heads have a maximum capacity of $^{13}/_{16}$ inch.

Begin by putting a cutter on the arbor (3–10). Make sure the teeth are pointing toward you and that the appropriate side of the cutter is out. Many cutters will be marked "This Side Out" on one side; this designates the side that is closer to the arbor washers.

Add chippers as necessary to make the dado stack the appropriate width (3–11). Remember, the outer cutter is ⅛ inch. If an odd-sized dado is being made, a plastic or cardboard washer can be inserted between the cutters and chippers to set a specific width.

Mount the last cutter (3–12). Stagger the chippers between the cutters so that the carbide tips do not contact each other. The chippers next to the cutters should be positioned so that their tips are in the gullets of the cutters. This will prevent damage to the tips and ensure an accurate setting. This also balances the head as it turns.

Put the arbor washer and arbor nut on the arbor and tighten the arbor nut. The dado stack should be held between the thumb and index finger (3–13). Force should be applied to the wrench until the dado stack can no longer be held; this will be tight enough. The nut will tighten some more on saws with left-hand threads. *(Note: If all the threads of the arbor nut do not engage with threads on the arbor, remove the arbor washer and replace the arbor nut. This should result in total thread engagement. It is not safe to run a dado head unless all the threads of the arbor nut are engaged with threads on the arbor.)*

Once these tasks have been accomplished, the final setup can be made. See the following sections for information on making the final setup.

MOUNTING AN ADJUSTABLE DADO HEAD

An adjustable dado head consists of one or two blades centered in a hub. To adjust the dado head to cut a particular width, the hub is turned with the blades(s) remaining still. This adjustment is made with the power disconnected. An indicator line on the hub reveals what size will be cut with any settings.

Mount the dado head on the arbor (3–14). Make sure that the flat side of the tooth is pointing toward you when you are at the front of the saw. With some adjustable dado heads, a sleeve is mounted on the arbor before the dado head can be mounted. Be careful not to change the adjustment while mounting the dado head.

Now the arbor washer and arbor nut are mounted. If all the threads of the arbor nut do not engage with the arbor, remove the washer and replace the nut. If all the threads of the arbor nut do not engage with the arbor, do not use the adjustable dado head on the saw. *For a safe setup, all threads of the arbor nut must be engaged with the arbor.* Some saws have a short arbor. The only dado head that may be used on those saws is a stack dado. Take no chances when setting up any table saw!

Tighten the arbor nut by holding the blade between the thumb and index finger while turning the wrench. When you can no longer hold the blade, the arbor nut is tight enough.

The next step consists of making the final setup. Refer to the following section for information on this.

FINAL SETUP

Install the dado head throat plate (3–15). Be sure that it is fastened correctly in place. Some throat

3–10. *Placing a cutter on the arbor. The flat face of the tooth should point toward the table-saw operator at the top of the blade.*

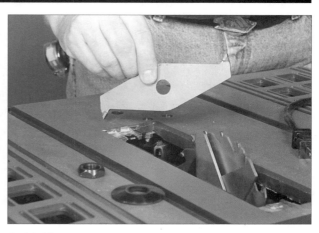

3–11. *The chippers are staggered around the arbor to balance the dado head. The carbide tips on the chipper closest to the cutter are in the gullets of the cutter. This prevents any damage to the carbide and makes the setting more accurate.*

3–12. *Position the last cutter on the arbor. Match the gullets on the cutter to the carbide tips on the chipper nearest to the cutter.*

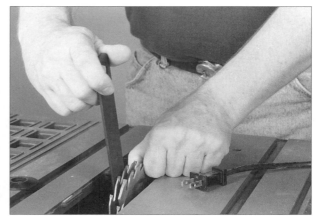

3–13. *When the arbor nut is being tightened, the dado stack should be held between the thumb and index finger, and the arbor nut tightened until the dado head cannot be held. That will be tight enough. All threads of the arbor nut should be engaged with the arbor. Do not operate the dado head if this is not the case.*

3–14 (left). *Before the adjustable dado head is mounted to the arbor, the sleeve is put on the arbor, if one is used.*

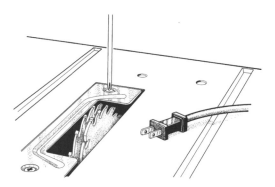

3–15. Replace the regular throat plate with a dado throat plate. Tighten the screws securely.

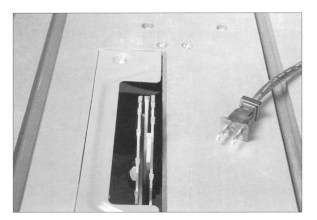

3–16. Make sure that the dado head does not contact the throat plate. Turn the dado head over by hand to be sure.

plates are held by gravity; others are screwed in place or held by a spring clip. Turn the dado head over by hand to be sure that it does not contact the throat plate (3–16). If it does contact the throat plate, this may be because it is the wrong throat plate. Consult the manufacturer's specifications if there is a problem.

Plug in the saw and prepare to make a test cut in a true, defect-free scrap. Use the miter gauge to control the stock. Set the dado height to no more than ⅜ inch above the table. The fence will not be on the saw.

Turn on the saw. Grip the miter gauge, hold-

ing the stock securely. Guide the miter gauge forward slowly. When the dado is cut (3–17), retract the miter gauge and stock. Shut off the saw and let the dado head come to complete stop. Check the dado for width and length. Make any needed adjustments and recheck the setup.

Note: A splitter-mounted guard cannot be used for dado operations. Refer to the illustrations in the following sections on cutting dadoes to learn how to set up for a safe dadoing operation. Work carefully, keeping hands clear of the dado head. Once the dadoing operation is complete, replace the guard immediately.

3–17. Make a trial cut to determine that the setup is correct. Make any needed adjustments.

Common Dadoes

Dado cuts are made in a manner similar to ripping, crosscutting, and mitering operations. (These techniques are described in Chapter 5.) When the dado goes the long way in sheet stock or with the grain in solid stock (refer to 3–1), the dadoing process is like a rip cut in which the fence is used. A dado cut across solid stock or the short way on a piece of sheet stock is similar to a crosscut in which a miter gauge is used to control the operation. Any dado going diagonally across the grain is similar to a miter cut in which the gauge is used to control the stock and the angle of cut.

PRELIMINARY SETUP

Before proceeding with the dado cuts, the dado width and height should be set correctly. Follow the procedures for a trial cut discussed in Final Setup on pages 52 and 54.

DADOES WITH THE GRAIN

When a dado is cut with the grain, the first setup consists of positioning the fence. This is determined by the location of the dado from the edge of the workpiece. Set the distance from the fence to the edge of the dado head so that it is equal to the distance of the dado to the edge of the stock (3–18). If working with an adjustable dado head, rotate the dado head until you find a tooth that is closest to the fence. Use this tooth to set the fence. Make this setting with the power disconnected. Lock the fence securely in position.

Put the work against the fence and move it up to the dado head. Check the setting with the workpiece. The layout line will touch the edge of the dado head when the edge of the piece touches the fence. If the setting lines up, the cut can be made. Make the needed adjustments if the setting is not correct.

A WORD ABOUT DADO CUTS	Most dado cuts can be made in a single setting if they are

less than ⅜ inch deep and ½ inch wide. Some table saws do not have enough power to make this cut, so a shallower cut is made first. A second cut at the desired depth completes the cut.

The hardness of the wood can also be a factor. Some woods such as rock maple resist cutting and require lighter cuts. Forcing stock against a dado head can only lead to a hand slipping into the dado head. Stay in control of the stock by taking appropriate cuts. This will result in better cuts and a safer environment.

3–18. The distance from the fence to the edge of the stock determines the position of the dado head.

3–19. The dado cut should be made as though it were a rip cut. Hands should be kept clear of the dado head. The featherboard helps control the workpiece.

Featherboards can be clamped to the table saw and/or fence to help control stock while the dado is being cut. Make sure they are clamped securely.

Turn on the saw and make the cut (3–19). Use a push stick to control the stock and keep hands away from the dado head. Push the stock completely past the dado head. Shut off the saw and let the dado head come to a complete stop before retrieving the piece. Never reach over a moving dado head to retrieve stock. This could cause serious injury.

DADOES ACROSS THE GRAIN

Dadoes cut across the grain are controlled with the miter gauge. A wooden face can be attached to the miter gauge to achieve greater control. The auxiliary face should extend beyond the dado head. This will help in positioning stock for dadoing (3–20). A stop can also be clamped to the auxiliary face. This will ensure that multiple parts are cut uniformly.

Once stock is positioned against the miter gauge and away from the dado head (3–21), the saw can be turned on. Guide the miter gauge and stock into the dado head (3–22). Do not force the stock or feed it too quickly. When the dado is completed, retract the stock and miter gauge. Hold the piece securely against the miter gauge while retracting it. Any twisting of the workpiece could result in binding and a possible kickback.

DADOES AT AN ANGLE

A dado can be cut at an angle by turning the miter gauge or by tilting the dado head. If the dado head is tilted, the methods described will be used. Be certain that the dado head does not contact the throat plate when the dado is tilted. Disconnect the power and turn the head over by hand to be certain that this is not a problem.

When the miter gauge is turned to a specific angle, the dado is cut using the process described above for dadoes cut across the grain (3–23). Make sure that the miter-gauge setting is accurate and that the head is locked securely. A stop can control the position of the stock (3–24). The quality of the dado cut depends on feed speed, wood, hardness, and the sharpness of the dado head (3–25).

DADOES ACROSS THE GRAIN

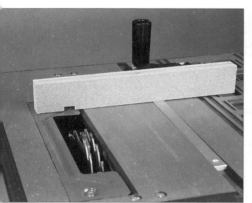

3–20. This auxiliary face has a layer of abrasive on it that increases the friction and control over the work. The dado cut into the face helps position the workpiece accurately.

3–21. The stock is positioned against the auxiliary face attached to the miter gauge. This cut should be made in the same manner as a crosscut.

3–22. The stock should be held securely as the miter gauge is pushed forward.

3–23. This special auxiliary face has been attached to the miter gauge. The miter gauge has been turned to the desired angle.

3–24. The stop on the auxiliary face locates the workpiece. Push the miter gauge forward, holding the work securely against the auxiliary face. Retract the miter gauge when the cut is complete, and then shut off the saw.

3–25. The quality of the dado cut depends on the sharpness of the dado head, the hardness of the wood, the depth of cut, and the feed speed. The best way to discover how to get the best results from a dado head is experience.

Rabbet Joints

A rabbet joint (refer to 3–2) can be cut using a dado head. This requires an auxiliary wooden fence. Part of the dado head is actually housed in the auxiliary fence. The opening for the dado head is cut by raising the moving dado head into the auxiliary wooden fence.

The process begins by lowering the dado head beneath the table. Next, set up the dado head. Disconnect the power during the setup. Attach a ¾ to 1-inch-thick wood fence to the metal fence (3–26). This fence should be about the same length and width as the metal fence. It is normally attached to the left side of the fence. Use wood screws to attach the fence.

Mark a pencil line on the wood fence indicating the approximate rabbet depth (3–27). Make the mark above the position of the dado head. Move the wood auxiliary fence into position over the dado head. Make sure that at least ⅛ inch of the wood fence nearest to the metal fence is clear of the dado head and will not be cut. Lock the fence in position. Turn on the saw and raise the dado head into the fence. Keep an eye on the layout line. Continue raising the dado head until you cut into the line (3–28). Shut off the dado head and let it come to a complete stop. Readjust the dado depth and fence position to the desired rabbet size.

When edge rabbets are cut, the stock will ride along the edge of the auxiliary fence. A featherboard can be used to control the stock; use a push stick to guide the piece (3–29). A piece of stock may also be secured to the auxiliary fence above the dado head to act as a barrier guard. End rabbets are cut using a miter gauge to control the stock (3–30). The end grain rides on the auxiliary fence as the rabbet is cut.

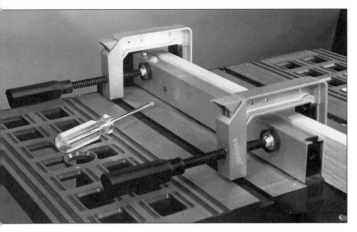

3–26. *Attach an auxiliary fence to the fence with wood screws.*

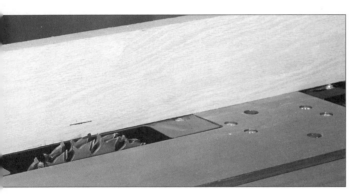

3–27. *Mark a pencil line on the auxiliary fence at the rabbet depth (usually ⅜ inch).*

3–28. *Raise the dado head until the pencil line is cut. Shut off the saw and allow the blade to stop before making any adjustments.*

3–29. *Cutting an edge rabbet. A featherboard, a piece of stock that acts as a barrier, and a push stick make this operation safer.*

3–30. *Cutting an end rabbet using the miter gauge and fence to control the cut.*

Lap Joints and Tenons

Lap joints (3–31) and tenons (3–32) are cut in a similar fashion when a dado head is used. A lap joint is simply a large end rabbet. It is cut on one face only and mates to an identical piece. A tenon has an end rabbet on each face. Each rabbet is about one-third the thickness of the workpiece.

The procedure for both tenons and lap joints is similar. First, determine how long the lap joint or

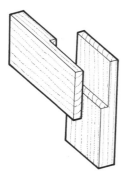

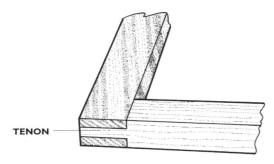

3–31. Lap joints, which are basically large end rabbets, can be cut with a dado head.

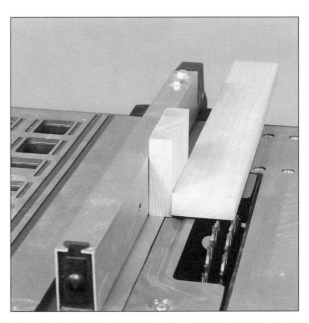

TENON

3–32. The tenon is the horizontally positioned part of this through mortise-and-tenon joint.

tenon is to be. Generally, it is equal to the width of the mating part, plus ¹⁄₁₆ inch. The ¹⁄₁₆-inch allowance makes the joint easier to sand and clean up.

The next step is to locate the shoulder of the lap joint. This requires a stop (3–33). A stop clamped to the fence can position the stock for the first cut. A stop clamped to the table or to an auxiliary face on the miter gauge will also work. The stop ensures that there will be no wedging action when the first dado cut is made.

The dado height is now set. For lap joints, it is set at the centerline on the stock. This is because the joint is a mirror image of itself. Check the dado setting on a piece of scrap wood before beginning. The dado height for a tenon is one-third the thickness of the stock. Make a test setup in scrap to determine if the height is correct.

The cutting can begin now. Butt the workpiece against the stop and guide the stock forward, holding it firmly against the miter gauge (3–34). Complete the first dado and retract the miter gauge and workpiece (3–35). Move the stock away from the stop one width of the dado head and make another cut (3–36). Continue this process until the stock is removed. Shut off the saw and allow it to come to a complete stop. Test the fit of the lap joint to its mate (3–37).

If a tenon is being made, turn the piece over and make the same cuts on the opposite face. Again, work away from the stop (3–38). This is the safest way, because your hands are moving away from, *not toward*, the dado.

The tenon requires a mortise as its mate (3–39). The process for making a mortise is found in the following section. Refer to it if you wish to make a through mortise.

3–33. Making a lap joint. A stop is used to position the stock. The lap joint is equal to the stock width or is slightly greater. The excess can be used for trimming or cleanup. The lap joint shown here is a corner lap joint.

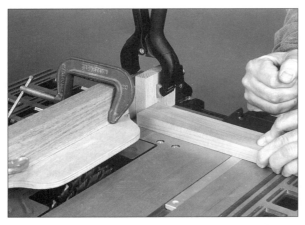

3–34. *The stock is butted to the stop, and then the miter gauge is pushed forward while the stock is held firmly.*

3–35. *The miter gauge is retracted after the cut is completed.*

3–36. *The stock is moved away from the stop a distance equal to the width of the dado head, and another cut is made.*

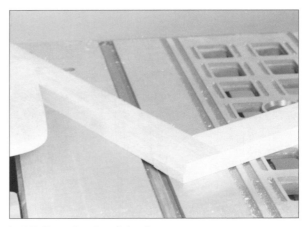

3–37. *Test the fit of the lap joint to its mate.*

3–38. *Making a tenon. The cuts shown in 3–33 to 3–36 for a lap joint are made on the opposite face of the stock.*

3–39. *A mortise must be made to fit the tenons. Refer to Through Mortises on pages 61 and 62 for information on making mortises.*

Also refer to Lap Joints on pages 101 and 102 for information on making lap joints with a single blade and Making a Frame with Lap Joints on pages 119 to 121 for information on using lap joints to make a door frame.

Through Mortises

The through mortise (refer to 3–32) requires support during the cut. This is because the dado head removes a large amount of material and because the piece is positioned vertically for cutting. The best support and control for this cut comes from a tenoning jig.

Set the tenoning jig in the miter-gauge slot or over the fence and secure the workpiece in the jig. Make sure the work is perpendicular to the table. Adjust the base of the tenoning jig so that the dado head is positioned to cut away the waste material. A tenon can be used for adjustment (3–40). Clamp the jig securely at the setting so the cut can be made.

In some cases, the dado head will have to be adjusted to a specific width in order to make the mortise in one cut. Test cuts in scrap stock will determine when the dado head is set correctly. In other cases, the dado head is intentionally assembled so that it will make a cut that is smaller then the desired mortise. The mortise is then formed by making two separate cuts. When two cuts are necessary, the dado head is aligned with one edge of the mortise. The second cut can be made by reversing the workpiece in the tenoning jig.

After the workpiece is positioned relative to the dado head, the height of the head must be set. This cut should also be tested on scrap. When adjusting the height, it is better to set it slightly low. This way, it can be raised slowly to the desired height.

A guard cannot be used on this cut, so it is important that the hands be positioned on the tenoning jig. A barrier can be clamped to the table to prevent contact with the dado head. This will keep hands clear of the rotating dado head. Position the tenoning jig so that the stock is clear of the dado head. Turn on the saw. Position your hands on the tenoning jig and guide it into the dado head (3–41). If the dado loses speed, the

3–40 (right). Making a through mortise. The tenon can be used to lay out the mortise. The dado head should line up with the tenon.

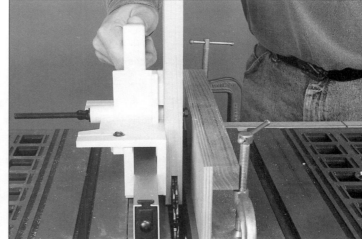

3–41. The work should be guided into the dado head. Hands should be kept on the jig.

feed rate is too fast. If the feed rate is too slow, there may be burning. Experience will determine the correct feed speed for various wood species. After the cut is complete, pull the tenoning jig back to you and shut off the saw. Let the blade come to a complete stop before releasing the work from the tenoning jig.

If a second cut is required, reverse the piece in the tenoning jig and clamp it securely. Repeat the process on all pieces. Check the fit to the mating piece (3–42). Make any needed adjustments.

3–42. Check the fit between the mating tenon and mortise. If they have to be forced together, the fit is too tight.

Box or Finger Joints

Finger or box joints are corner joints made up of mating fingers and spaces (3–43). A dado cut in the wood forms the space, and the wood on either side of the space becomes the finger. The mating corner pieces slip together to form a strong joint. Each finger and space cut reveals more edge grain. This increases the amount of edge-grain gluing surface. The edge-to edge-glue joint is one of the strongest. In addition, the increased amount of glue surface makes the joint stronger by the volume of gluing surface.

Finger joints are cut using a commercial or user-made jig (3–44 and 3–45). (Also refer to Making Box Joints with a User-Made Jig, which follows.) Usually, the jig is attached to the miter gauge or controlled by the miter-gauge slot. In some cases, the jig is designed to be attached to the fence. Fingers are usually no wider than stock thickness. Fingers cut in ½-inch stock would be ½ inch wide or less. Narrower fingers look nicer, but take longer to cut and increase the chance of error. When narrower fingers are cut, there is a better chance that each finger would be cut .001 inch wider

3–43. A box joint is made up of mating fingers and spaces. Most of the glue joint is face grain. A box joint is one of the strongest joints.

3–44. This commercial jig can be used to make finger joints. It attaches to the miter gauge.

3–45. This user-made jig can also be used to make finger joints. It, too, is attached to the miter gauge.

or narrower than needed. For example, if ten cuts were made on the end of the board, the last cut would be .010 inch off. This error could cause fitting problems.

After deciding on a finger width, set up the dado head or saw blade to cut that width. Adjust the dado height to slightly greater than stock thickness. This will allow a small amount to be sanded off the fingers after assembly, and ensures flush, square joints.

MAKING BOX JOINTS WITH A USER-MADE JIG

Inexpensive commercial jigs are available to make box joints, but the jig can also be user-made. Select a piece of stock six to eight inches wide and 12 to 16 inches long. Cut a dado through the edge of the piece about six inches from one end. (Refer to Common Dadoes on pages 54 to 57.) Measure the dado width and record the measurement. Mark off a space equal to the measurement next to the dado. Insert a piece of stock into the dado and glue it in position. The piece should extend about one inch beyond the front of the dadoed piece. Once the glue cures, the insert will control the spacing of the fingers. Commercial jigs have a pin to control spacing.

Position the jig on the saw table with the insert to the right of the dado head. The distance from the

dado head to the insert should be equal to the width of the dado. Once the position is correct, the jig can be attached to the miter gauge with wood screws.

Lay out the pieces that will be cut. Set them on edge the way they will fit together. Determine which pieces start with a finger and which pieces start with a cut, and mark them on the edge with an "F" or a "C" (3–46). It is good technique to start all the long pieces with a cut. Start all the cuts and fingers from the appearance edge; that way, any partial fingers or cuts will be at the bottom of the box.

Place the "F" piece against the insert with the piece on the dado head side of the jig (3–47 and 3–48). Position the stock flat on the table and against the insert. Turn on the saw and guide the stock and jig into the dado head. Hold the stock securely (3–49). Hands should be kept clear of the dado head. Special user-made guard devices can be added to make the operation safer (3–50). After the cut is complete, pull the jig and work back toward you. Place the cutout area in the workpiece over the spacer and repeat the cutting process. Continue this process until all of the parts starting with a finger are cut (3–51).

Pieces beginning with a cutout are now cut. Place a finger over the insert with the work to

BOX JOINTS WITH A USER-MADE JIG

3–46. Once the pieces for the finger joints have been cut and laid out properly mark their edges with an "F" or a "C." Then begin the cut. The pieces marked "F" begin with a finger.

(continued on following page)

3–47. *The "F" piece placed against the stop. The piece is on the dado head side of the jig.*

3–48. *The stock rests on the base with the "F" piece. The piece is on the blade side of the stop.*

3–49. *Hold the stock securely while guiding the miter gauge forward. A clamp can help hold the stock.*

3–50. *Special user-made barriers or guards can be added to make this operation safer.*

3–51. *Continue cutting until both ends of each piece have been cut from edge to edge.*

3–52. *The "F" piece is now placed against the stop. The entire piece is now on the side away from the dado. The "C" piece is now butted against the other part.*

(continued on following page)

the right of the insert. Place the cutout area next to the finger (3–52). Both pieces should be rest-

ing on the table or jig. Turn on the saw and hold both pieces securely. Guide the pieces and jig

BOX JOINTS WITH A USER-MADE JIG (CONTINUED)

3–53. The finger acts as a spacer while the cut is formed on the edges where the letter C appears.

3–54. After the first cut is made on both ends of the parts, the cut area is butted to the stop for the next cut.

3-55. Move slowly when making the cuts. This will reduce tear-out.

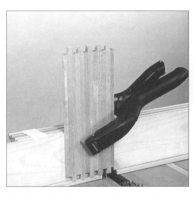

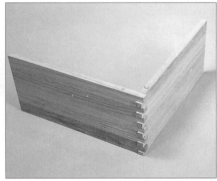

3–56. Continue cutting until both ends have been cut.

3–57. Test the fit between the parts. It is good practice to make trial cuts until you are sure the fit is correct.

3–58. Fit the parts together without using glue. If they have to be forced to fit, they are too tight and will be impossible to glue together.

into the dado head. Retract the jig and pieces after the cut is complete. Make the first cut on all pieces with the finger as a spacer (3–53).

Once all the first cuts are complete, the finger part is removed from the jig. The cut area is then butted against the insert (3–54) and a dado cut is made (3–55). The piece is moved so the dado is over the insert, and another dado is cut. This process is repeated until all of the parts have been cut (3–56).

Test the fit between the mating parts and dry-fit the box (3–57 and 3–58). The parts should not have to be forced together. If so, the position of the jig has to be adjusted. If the fingers are bigger than the cuts, the jig has to be moved toward the dado head one-half the difference between the finger and cut.

If a uniform cut is not being produced, the pieces may be moving. Try clamping the pieces to the jig. Also, make sure the throat plate is even with the table; if it is not, some cuts will be deeper than others. The jig described in this section compensates for this problem by allowing the work to ride on the base.

Drawer Corner Joints

The drawer corner joint is similar to a rabbet corner joint (refer to Rabbets on pages 90 to 94), except there is a tongue on the drawer front that slips into a mating dado in the drawer side for greater strength and rigidity (3–59).

Begin by setting the dado head up for a ¼-inch dado cut. Test the setup in a piece of scrap. Attach a wood face to the fence. It should be ¾ inch thick, about five to eight inches wide, and as long as the fence. Use screws to hold it in place. Set the distance between the fence and dado head to a dimension equal to the cut made by the dado head. Set the dado height to about ¹⁄₃₂ inch greater than the thickness of the drawer side.

Butt the drawer front to the wood face on the fence. The inside of the drawer front should be touching the wood face, and the end should be touching the table. Place a straight piece of stock on top of the fence and clamp the drawer front to it (3–60). This will control the workpiece.

Turn on the saw and guide the drawer front into the dado head (3–61). Keep the straight edge on top of the fence and the back of the drawer against the fence. Make the dado cut in the drawer front and shut off the saw. Turn the drawer front over and position it so the other end is on the table. Make sure the inside of the

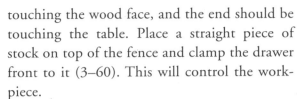

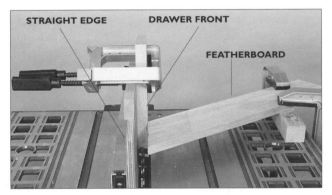

3–60. Butt the inside face of the drawer front to the fence. The end should touch the table. Clamp a straightedge to it. This will ride on top of the fence and hold the drawer front in position.

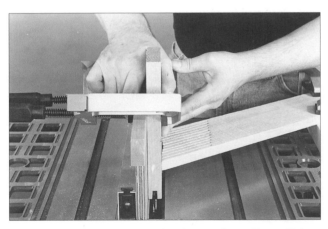

3–59. The drawer corner joint consists of a tongue on the drawer front and a mating dado on the drawer side.

3–61. Make a dado cut in the drawer front. Shut off the saw. Remove the piece when the dado head stops turning.

drawer front touches the auxiliary face. Make the dado cut in the end and shut off the saw (3–62).

Lower the dado head for a ¼-inch-deep cut; do not change the position of the fence. Make a dado cut on the inside face of the drawer sides (3–63). Put the good face down and butt the front to the fence. The rear edge will be touching the miter gauge. Turn on the saw and make the dado cut along the front of both sides. Remember, the right and left sides are not the same; instead, they are mirror images of each other. If the groove for the drawer bottom has not been cut, they are still interchangeable.

The sides should now fit with the front (3–64). The tongue on the front should fit the dado in the drawer side, and the stock in front of the tongue should fit the groove in the drawer front. The tongue will initially prevent the drawer side from fitting into the front correctly, so it will have to be trimmed.

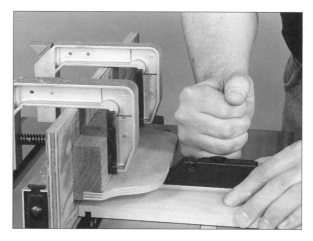

3–63. With the dado height at ¼ inch, cut a dado on the inside face of the drawer sides. The front of the drawer side should touch the fence. Remember, the drawer sides are mirror images of each other. Be careful when positioning them for the cut. If the drawer groove has been cut, it will be close to the miter gauge on one side and away from the miter gauge for the mating cut.

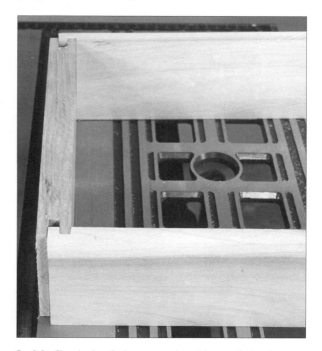

3–64. Check the fit between the sides and the front. The tongues on the front must be trimmed. The open distance between the parts is equal to the amount that must be removed from the tongues.

3–62. Make the same cut on the opposite end. Make sure that the inside face of the drawer front is against the fence.

The distance between the face of the drawer front and the bottom of the groove on the drawer front is the same as the amount of material that must be removed from the tongues on the drawer front. Use a saw blade to trim the tongues. Make sure the blade height is set low; if not, you could cut into the drawer front (3–65 and 3–66).

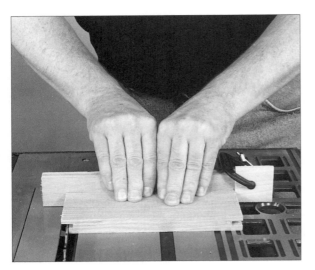

3–65. Trim the tongues to length. A stop can be used to position them. Double-check the blade height. Do not cut into the drawer front.

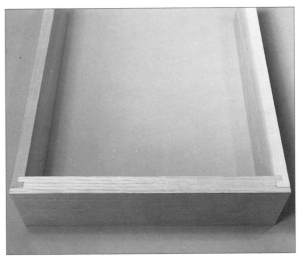

3–66. The pieces should fit together as shown here when the parts have been trimmed correctly.

CHAPTER 4

Lumber and Sheet Stock Cutting Techniques

This chapter discusses guidelines for cutting lumber and sheet stock. The table saw can also be used to cut plastic laminates. Refer to Chapter 6 (pages 113 to 116) for information on this.

Lumber Cutting Techniques

The lumber bought from a lumber dealer is usually a softwood (such as pine and fir) with true faces and edges. It has been processed for house framing, but it can be cut into shorter or narrower pieces. These cuts would be made at the table saw.

The true face and edge are used as the control surfaces when the lumber is being cut on a table saw. The control surfaces should always be in contact with the table and the fence or miter gauge.

Lumber, as all other types of wood, has three dimensions: thickness, width, and length. The dimensions of all wood pieces are discussed in this order. For example, a 2 x 4 that is eight feet long is considered two inches thick, four inches wide, and eight feet long. However, these are the nominal (rough) dimensions before the piece is dressed or smoothed. That 2 x 4 bought from the lumber dealer would actually be about 1½ inches thick and 3½ inches wide.

Hardwood lumber (such as maple and oak) must also be dressed or smoothed on one edge and one face before it can be cut on a table saw. Hardwood lumber is usually sold as random widths and lengths. This requires more careful selection and planning when using hardwoods. Most hardwood is used for furniture fabrication. It is usually more expensive than softwood. Hardwood is usually harder than softwood and has greater resistance to sawing.

Make sure that the hardwood or softwood lumber being cut on the table saw is true and free of defects, such as loose knots and splits or checks. These defects can contribute to kickbacks and other problems.

It is also important that the cut be made with a blade designed for the particular application, and one which has the proper pitch. Refer to Material/Blade Guidelines to determine which blade would be appropriate when cutting softwood, hardwood, sheet stock, and plastic laminates.

Sheet Stock Cutting Techniques

Sheet stock is another form of wood commonly cut on a table saw. Sheet stock is a generic term for any re-manufactured wood product, such as plywood, hardboard, particleboard, oriented

MATERIAL/BLADE GUIDELINES

Dimensional softwood under 1" thick	40-to-50-tooth blade
Dimensional softwood over 1½" thick	40-to-50-tooth crosscut blade
Hardwood up to 1" thick	40-to-50-tooth crosscut or rip blade
Hardwood 1 to 2" thick	40-to-50-tooth crosscut blade or 24-tooth rip blade
Plywood and other sheet stock	60-tooth blade
Plastic laminates	60-to-80-tooth triple-chip blade. Refer to Chapter 6.

strand board, and paneling. (See Sheet Stock Overview.) These products are sold in sheets from 48 inches to 60 inches wide and from 96 inches to 120 inches long. These sheets have true edges and faces. In some cases, they have grain like a piece of lumber, and in other cases they have no grain pattern.

Plywood and other sheet stock are cut in the same way as solid stock. When cutting the long way, a rip cut is made (4–1). (Refer to Chapter 5 for information on making rip cuts with a single blade.) Cuts the long way in sheet stock are controlled by the fence.

When cutting across the piece, a crosscut is usually made (4–2). (Refer to Chapter 5 for information on making crosscuts with a single blade.) Cuts across smaller pieces are controlled with the miter gauge.

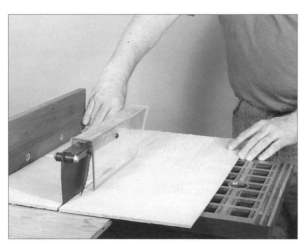

4–1. When plywood or other sheet stock is being cut the long way, a rip cut is made.

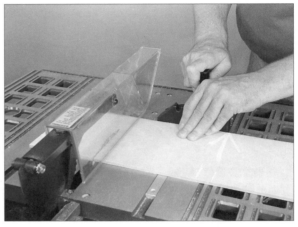

4–2. When a cut is being made across plywood or other sheet stock, a crosscut is usually made.

The biggest danger when cutting sheet stock is when the operator makes a rip cut to a square piece using the fence. If the piece twists, it is likely to rise over the blade and kick back. (See Preventing Kickback on pages 72 to 74.) A splitter reduces the likelihood of a kickback because the piece cannot twist and lift onto the blade. Never attempt any cut without two control surfaces, such as the table and miter gauge, or the table and fence. Freehand cutting—in which only the table is used to control the cut—usually results in disaster.

Planning is essential to cutting sheet stock. Observe the following guidelines:

1. Make cuts that reduce overall size first (4–3). A long cut may actually make two pieces that are easier to manage. A portable circular saw can also be used to reduce the size of the sheet stock.

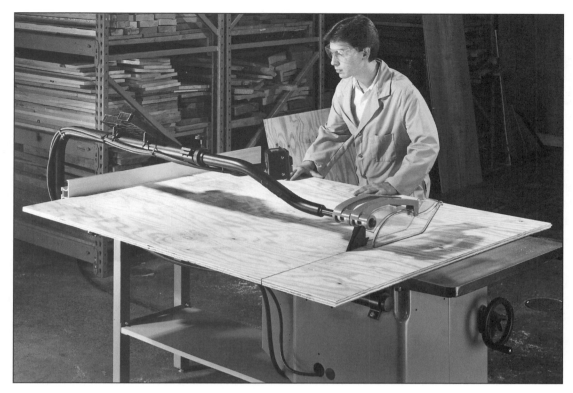

4–3. *Make cuts that reduce the stock's overall size first.*

2. Use factory edges as control surfaces (4–4). The outside edges are true and square. Positioning them against the fence or miter gauge ensures that the cuts will be truer.

3. Make a scale drawing of the cuts and number them (4–5). This ensures that the work will be done efficiently and will reduce the chance of errors.

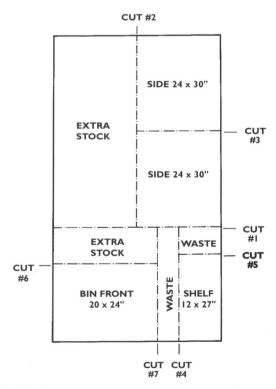

4–5. *Before cutting sheet stock, make a scale drawing designating the cuts and number them. This practice will make cutting more efficient and reduce waste.*

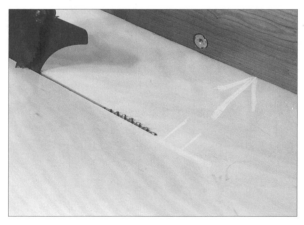

4–4. *Factory edges are true and square. Put them against the fence or miter gauge to ensure the most accurate cut.*

SHEET STOCK OVERVIEW

Hardboard is made by reducing wood chips to wood fibers and lignin (the natural glue in wood) through boiling and then pressing them into sheets. Common sheet sizes range from ⅛ to 1 inch in thickness. Hardboard is dimensionally stable, is highly resistant to wear, bends easily, and does not splinter when sawed. It is used for drawer bottoms, panel backing, and siding and cabinet parts.

Medium-Density Fiberboard (MDF), available in thickness from ½ to 1 inch, is used for most home furniture and cabinetwork.

Oriented Strand Board is sheet stock made of relatively large pieces of wood that have been formed into sheets. Water-resistant, it is used primarily in building construction because of its rough exterior.

Paneling is sheet stock used to decorate walls of a home. Most panel stock is made of plywood, particleboard, or hardboard, and is is usually ³⁄₁₆ to ½ inch thick. It may be designed for interior or exterior use.

Particleboard is made from wood chips that are mixed with glue and pressed into sheets. It is very stable dimensionally. Commonly available in thickness of ½, ⅝, and ¾ inch, it is used often as a backing material for veneer and plastic laminates.

Plywood consists of layers or plies of wood that are glued together in a sandwich-like fashion. Because the grain on the plies alternates in different directions, plywood is dimensionally stable. It will not expand as much as solid wood with similar dimensions. Its drawbacks include unsightly edges and a reduced ability to hold screws and nails driven into the edges. Hardwood plywood is used for appearance purposes on furniture and casework. Softwood plywood is used for general and furniture construction.

4–6. *The best blades to use to cut sheet stock are alternate top bevel (as shown here) and triple-chip carbide-tipped blades that have 40 to 60 teeth.*

4. If the sheet stock has grain, make sure that the grain is oriented correctly on the parts being cut.

In some cases, specialty blades are selected for cutting sheet stock. Do not use tool-steel blades. Some sheet stock is made of glues and materials that will take the edge off tool-steel blades in a single cut. Carbide-tipped blades work best (4–6).

The section Sheet Stock Overview describes different sheet-stock materials, their characteristics, and the purposes they are best suited for.

Preventing Kickback

One potential hazard that can occur whether solid wood or sheet stock is used is kickback.

A kickback occurs when a piece of stock is forced toward the operator at a great speed. Usually, the stock becomes trapped between the rotating blade and a stationary object such as the fence or guard. In some cases, the saw kerf or cut closes around the blade. This traps the blade.

Stock that is kicked back is being propelled at a very high speed. This is a serious hazard. Another hazard of the kickback is the fact that the operator's hand may be pulled into the blade as the stock kicks back. Using a guard will reduce the chance of this occurring.

Kickback hazards can be minimized by observing the following precautions. The reader should also refer to Chapter 10, which gives general safety instructions.

1. Cut only true, smooth stock that will not become twisted and pinched in the blade. Stock should have a minimum of two surfaces that are true and smooth—one face and one edge. Inspect the stock for loose knots. Avoid contacting loose knots with the blade.

2. Control all cuts with a miter gauge, fence, or jig. Never attempt to cut freehand (without any stock control). The stock will become twisted and kick back.

3. Use a guard equipped with a splitter. The splitter keeps the kerf open when stock is being cut.

4. Keep the anti-kickback pawls sharp. This allows them to dig into the wood if it begins to kick back. Use a file to bring them to a sharp point if they become dull.

5. Use only sharp, true blades. Dull or pitch-loaded blades are prone to kickbacks. Warped blades also tend to pinch in the kerf and cause kickbacks.

6. Remove the fence when crosscutting. Stock can be trapped between the blade and fence and will kick back, or up, as the cut is completed.

7. Make sure that the rip fence is parallel to the blade. When the fence is not parallel, stock may be pinched.

8. When making a rip cut, always feed the piece being cut completely through and past the blade. Never release the stock while it is still touching the blade and fence. A kickback may result. Use a push stick or push block for thin rip cuts.

9. Stand to the side of the saw when making a rip cut. Someone standing *behind* the piece being ripped may become the target of a kickback. Also, do not rip stock on the table saw without a guard or push stick. This can also cause a kickback or another potentially dangerous situation. As stock is fed into the blade, there is a tendency for the operator to reach over the blade. If the stock binds and, subsequently, kicks back, it will travel toward the operator. As the operator feels the tug on the workpiece, his reaction is to hold the work even more securely. The next thing the operator discovers is his hand on the saw blade. The piece may also continue backward toward the operator and cause further injury.

10. If a dado head is being used, do not reach over it to retrieve stock. Feed it completely past the blade with a push stick. Never pull the wood back toward you after the cut is made.

11. Always be aware of binding during a rip or crosscut. These cuts are always potential causes of kickback.

12. Always support long or heavy pieces. Control must be maintained over the work at all times.

13. Be as careful when cutting sheet stock as when cutting solid wood. Because sheet stock does not have the grain structure of solid wood, most woodworkers feel that a kickback is not likely. This is a false and dangerous assumption. Work carefully. Treat a crosscut in sheet stock the same way you would solid stock, and kickbacks will be minimized.

14. Never attempt to saw a piece that is longer than it is wide with the width against the fence. A piece sawn in this fashion is likely to wedge and kick back. The splitter will reduce the chance of wedging and kickback if it is in place.

5 Single-Blade Cutting Techniques

Rip Cuts

When a rip cut is made to reduce the width of a board, the cut is made with the grain of the board. Rip cuts are guided with the fence. The first step is to set the distance from the blade to the fence (5–1). Next, adjust the blade height to slightly greater than the stock thickness (about ⅛ inch) (5–2). For narrow rip cuts, the fence will interfere with the guard. For more information on narrow rip cuts, see the following section.

Once the distance from the blade to the fence has been set, the stock is positioned on the table with its true edge against the fence and its true face against the table. Position yourself to the side of the kickback zone (5–3). (The kickback zone is directly behind the blade.)

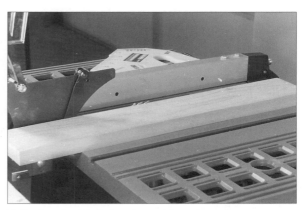

5–2. Set the blade height to ⅛ to ¼ inch greater than the thickness of the stock that will be ripped.

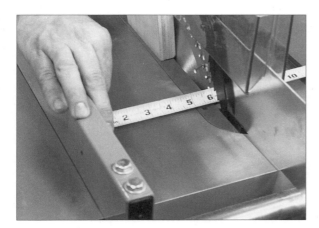

5–1. When making a rip cut, set the distance from the fence to the near side of the blade for the desired cut. Some table saws will have a scale on the front of the fence, but the method shown here is the most accurate.

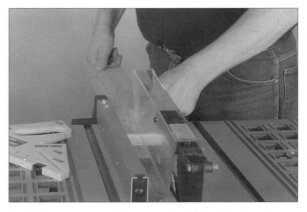

5–3. Position yourself to the side of the blade when making a rip cut. This will keep your body out of the kickback zone.

Next, the saw is turned on and stock is guided under the guard and into the blade (5–4). Keep the stock against the fence and table while feeding it forward (5–5). If the motor slows down, the stock is being fed too quickly. Long pieces of stock should be supported by a take-off table or other support. Guide the stock past the blade (5–6). If the rip width is less than four inches, use a push stick to control the wood. Shut off the saw and allow it to come to a complete stop.

Never reach over the blade to retrieve stock. This could result in a kickback or contact with the blade. The cutoff will remain stationary under the pressure of the guard and anti-kickback pawls (5–7).

Inspect the stock after cutting. If there are *burn* marks, it was either fed too slowly or the fence was not parallel to the blade. For information on alignment and adjustment, refer to Misaligned Table Saw on pages 32 to 34.

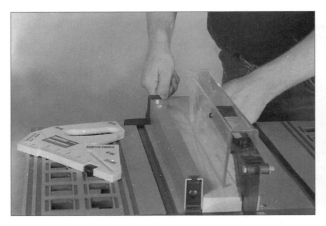

5–4. *The work is guided under the guard and into the turning blade. Be sure to keep the stock on the table and against the fence.*

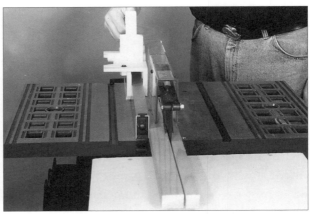

5–6. *Guide the stock completely past the blade before releasing it. The push stick shown here is actually mounted over the fence. It guides the stock and holds it down on the table.*

5–5. *Use a push stick to keep the stock against the fence. If the motor slows down, the stock is being fed too quickly.*

5–7. *The cutoff will remain stationary under the pressure of the guard and anti-kickback pawls. Do not try to retrieve the cutoff or step behind the blade until the blade has come to a complete stop.*

RIPPING THIN AND NARROW STOCK

Thin and narrow stock present additional problems when ripping. A thin piece of stock is lighter and prone to vibration. It tends to lift above the blade. Thin stock can also slip beneath the fence during a cut, causing binding (5–8). A narrow rip makes the use of a guard difficult. This is because the fence moves closer to the guard as the rip cut gets narrower.

To reduce chattering and vibration, one or

5–9. The L-shaped auxiliary fence attached to the fence makes narrow rip cuts possible with the guard in place.

5–8. On some saws, thin stock can actually slip beneath the fence. An auxiliary face on the fence can prevent this.

more featherboards can be clamped to an auxiliary wooden fence, which is secured to the metal fence. The featherboard has enough spring to keep the stock on the table during the cut. For some narrow rips, the guard may still be used. An auxiliary L-shaped fence is clamped to the metal fence (5–9). The distance from the auxiliary fence to the blade determines the ripping width. A matching push block rests on the horizontal piece of the fence while one edge rides along the vertical portion. The opposite edge has a pushing device that extends into the area

between the edge of the fence and blade. The pushing device guides the stock past the blade at the end of the cut (5–10 to 5–12). Avoid ripping pieces less than ½ inch wide. They could fall into the opening in the throat plate.

Make up a push block and fence as shown in 5–10 to 5–12. Set up the fence for the desired rip. Set the stock on the table and make the rip cut as outlined in Rip Cuts on pages 75 and 76. When coming to the end of the cut, hold the stock securely while putting the push block in place. Guide the push block forward; when it contacts the work, continue guiding it through the end of the rip cut. Be sure to guide the work and push block completely past the blade. In some cases, the push block cannot be retracted; the anti-kickback pawls stop its movement in the same way they would stop a kickback.

A featherboard may also be used to control thin stock when a guard is not used (5–13). This method requires that the guard be removed and that a featherboard be clamped to the fence or auxiliary fence immediately above the blade.

First, the rip width is set between the blade and fence (5–14). Next, the blade is dropped beneath the table and the stock is placed on the table against the fence. The featherboard is clamped over the blade path while it touches the stock. The feathers should be put under light tension to better hold the stock. This is accomplished by bending the feathers slightly (5–15).

Once the featherboard is clamped securely, the saw is turned on and the blade is raised into the work and featherboard; this keeps the feather-board from chattering as it is cut (5–16). Use one piece of stock to push the other as the piece approaches the featherboard (5–17).

Since there is no splitter, there is a greater chance of kickback with this method. Keep the stock under control at all times. When cutting is complete, hold the last piece securely after the last cut is made. Shut off the saw and allow it to come to a complete stop before releasing the last pushing piece and dismantling the setup. Be sure to replace the guard.

RIPPING THIN AND NARROW STOCK WITH A PUSH BLOCK AND FENCE

5–10. The distance from the blade to the edge of the plywood base determines the ripping width. A specialty push block (left) is ready to complete the cut.

5–11. The rip cut is completed using the push block. Notice how it goes under the guard without interference.

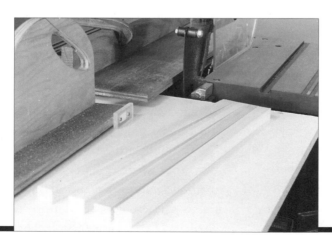

5–12. This technique allows narrow widths to be ripped uniformly with the guard in place.

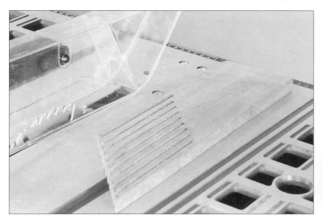

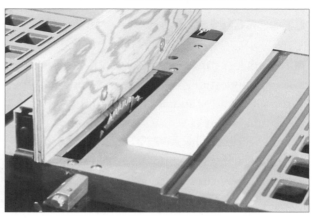

5–13. *This featherboard may be used to control thin stock during ripping. The technique for making a featherboard is found in Making a Featherboard on pages 26 to 28.*

5–14. *Set the rip width between the blade and fence. Then lower the blade beneath the table.*

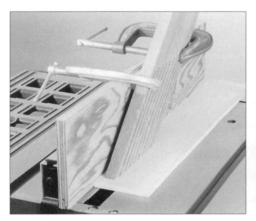

5–15. *Put the stock that will be ripped against the fence. Position the featherboard on the stock and over the blade. Bend the feathers slightly to put them under tension and clamp the featherboard to the fence.*

5–16. *Raise the blade through the work and into the featherboard. Guide the stock through the blade, keeping it against the fence. The featherboard holds the stock down and acts as a barrier between the operator and the blade.*

5–17. *Another piece of stock should be used to push the work through the blade. Continue cutting until enough ripped stock has been produced.*

Crosscuts

When stock is cut across the grain, it is crosscut. In most applications, the blade is perpendicular to the table and is square with the miter gauge. The blade height is set slightly greater than the stock thickness. The stock is positioned against the miter gauge. The cutting line is positioned so that the blade cuts in the waste portion of the wood (5–18).

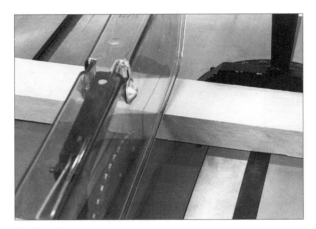

5–18. When making crosscuts, position the stock so that the blade is on the waste side of the layout line.

Guide the miter gauge with one hand and hold the stock against the miter gauge with the other. Push the miter gauge forward in the slot until cutting begins (5–19). Continue feeding at a moderate feed speed until the cut is complete (5–20). Shut off the saw and allow it to come to a complete stop before retrieving the piece or any cutoff (5–21). If the saw slows down during the cut, it is being fed too quickly.

It may be necessary to support long pieces when crosscutting. The extra weight can make control of the miter gauge difficult. There are many types of support devices (5–22 and 5–23). One of the most common is a piece of plywood clamped to a sawhorse. The edge of the plywood

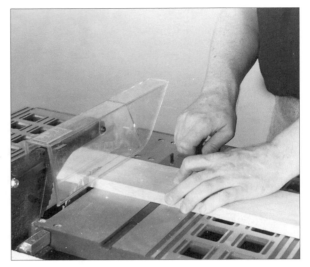

5–19. Hold the stock against the head of the miter gauge and guide the miter gauge forward. The stock will lift the guard, and the blade will begin the cut.

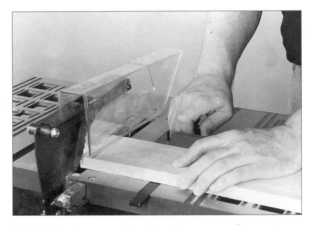

5–20. Continue moving the miter gauge forward until the cut is complete. The guard will hold the cutoff in place.

is even with the top of the saw table and supports the work.

When several pieces are being crosscut to the same length, an auxiliary face can be attached to the miter gauge and a clamp used to position a stop block. Another technique involves using the fence and a stop block.

The stop block, as shown in 5–24 and 5–25, is a piece of stock approximately two inches thick,

5–21. Retract the miter gauge and shut off the saw. Do not retrieve the cutoff until the blade has come to a complete stop.

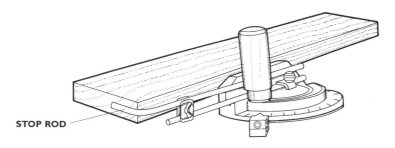

STOP ROD

5–22. Some stop rods attach to the miter gauge to control stock length when the stock is being crosscut or mitered. Be sure to keep the rods out of the blade's path. (Drawing courtesy of Sears Craftsman.)

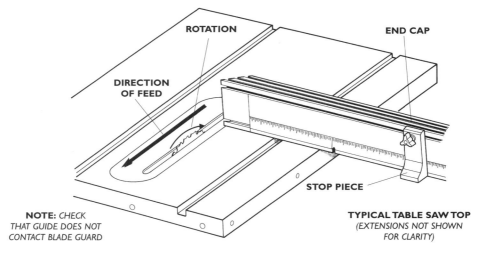

ROTATION

END CAP

DIRECTION OF FEED

STOP PIECE

NOTE: CHECK THAT GUIDE DOES NOT CONTACT BLADE GUARD

TYPICAL TABLE SAW TOP (EXTENSIONS NOT SHOWN FOR CLARITY)

5–23. This specialty attachment, which has an adjustable stop, can also control stock length. It can be attached to most miter gauges. (Drawing courtesy of Sears Craftsman.)

MAKING CROSSCUTS USING A STOP BLOCK

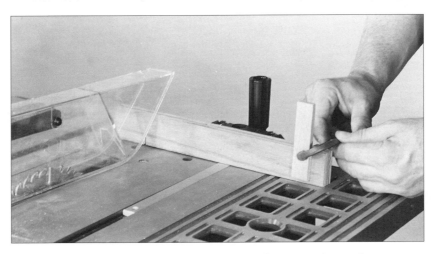

5–24. This auxiliary face has been attached to the miter gauge. A stop is clamped to it to control stock length.

5–25. The stock is butted against the auxiliary face. As the miter gauge is moved forward, the stock will be cut to the desired length.

two inches wide, and four inches long. The stop block is butted against the fence near the front of the table. The desired crosscut length is measured between the stop block and blade. The fence is locked at the setting and the stop block is moved to the infeed end of the fence and clamped in place. The stock can then be butted to the stop block and crosscut. The stop block positions the stock for the correct length. *Note: Never use the fence without a stop block when crosscutting. The cutoff will be trapped between the blade and fence. This will result in a kickback.*

Miter Cuts

Miter cuts are angular cuts made to the work. This section contains information on cutting face miters, end miters, edge miters and chamfers, and compound miters.

FACE MITERS

A face miter is an angular cut across the face of the workpiece (5–26). The face miter is often used for flat picture frames and door or window trim. Most face miters are cut at 45

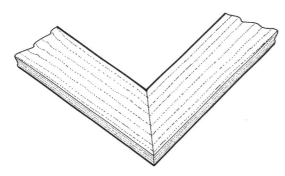

5–26. Face miter.

degrees, but other angles are cut when there are more than four sides. First, the blade must be square to the table; then the miter gauge must be adjusted to the desired angle. Drafting squares, sliding T-bevels (5–27), and protractors (5–28) can be used to set the angle. The layout tool is butted to the plate of the blade (keep it off the teeth). The other leg of the layout tool is butted to the head of the miter gauge while it is in the miter-gauge slot. Once the angle is set, the clamp knob is tightened.

The miter cut is made in a manner similar to a crosscut. (Refer to Crosscuts on pages 80 to 82.) The stock is positioned so that the blade is on the waste side. Move the stock and miter

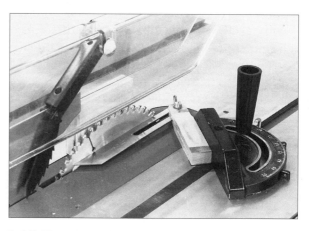

5–27. This sliding T-bevel can be used to transfer an angle from a piece that will be copied or from a protractor.

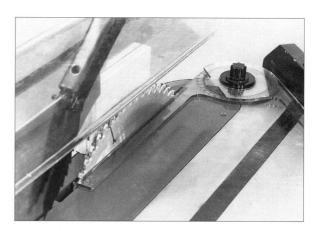

5–28. This protractor will help produce a very accurate miter layout. Keep the protractor against the plate of the blade.

gauge away from the blade. Turn on the saw and begin the cut (5–29). Hold the stock securely against the head of the miter gauge and push the miter gauge forward until the cut is complete. Retract the miter gauge and workpiece, holding them securely. Shut off the saw. Let the blade come to a complete stop before retrieving the cutoff (5–30).

In some cases, a wooden face is attached to the miter gauge. The face provides greater support for the work. Stops may also be clamped to the auxiliary face to control miter length (5–31). The cut made by the blade in the auxiliary face will enable the operator to position stock correctly for cutting. The auxiliary fence acts moves the cutoff away from the blade (5–32).

CUTTING FACE MITERS

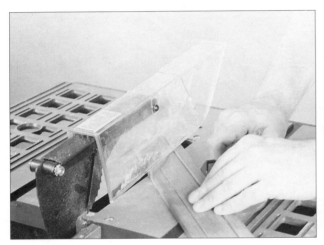

5–29. *When cutting a face miter, position the layout line relative to the blade. Keep the blade on the waste side of the line. Push the miter gauge forward, holding the stock against the table and miter gauge.*

5–30. *Shut off the saw and retract the miter gauge when the cut is complete. The cutoff is held in place by the guard to the left of the blade. These small cutoffs can be kicked back; be alert for any movement of the cutoff. Do not retrieve the cutoff until the blade has come to a complete stop.*

5–31. *This stop, which is clamped to the auxiliary face, controls the stock length during a miter cut.*

5–32. *The cut in the auxiliary face aids in positioning the stock for mitering. It also moves cutoffs away from the blade.*

END MITERS

Miters across the end of a piece of stock (5–33) are usually cut with the miter gauge set for 90 degrees (a crosscut) and the blade tilted to the desired angle (usually 45 degrees). Once the blade is tilted, the angle can be checked with a layout tool such as a miter square or sliding-T-bevel. Secure the blade at the desired angle. Make sure the blade is no more than ¼ inch above the stock; then lock the blade-height setting.

An end-miter cut is made in the same way as a crosscut. Position the cutting line so that the blade is in the waste portion of the workpiece. Hold the stock securely against the miter gauge and back the stock and the miter gauge away from the blade. Turn on the saw and push the miter gauge forward (5–34). Hold the stock securely and continue pushing forward until the cut is complete. Retract the miter gauge and stock. Shut off the saw and allow the blade to come to a complete stop before retrieving the cutoff (5–35).

CUTTING END MITERS

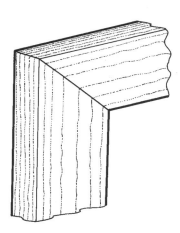

5–33. An end miter.

5–34. When an end miter is being cut, the blade has to be tilted to the desired angle and the stock positioned against the miter gauge and lined up with the blade.

5–35. Advance the miter gauge with the stock held securely against the head. When the cut is complete, retract the miter gauge. Shut off the saw; do not retrieve the cutoff until the blade has stopped.

EDGE MITERS AND CHAMFERS

An edge miter goes from face to face on a piece of stock at an angle (5–36). This cut is also known as a bevel. A cut that is similar to a bevel or end-miter cut is the chamfer. The chamfer cut goes from edge to edge, not face to face (5–37). Edge miters and chamfers are cut in the same manner. The only difference is the portion of the blade and fence used.

To make an edge-miter or chamfer cut, set the angle of the blade using the procedure described in End Miters. Make sure it is locked at the setting. Position the stock and fence. Make sure the blade is cutting in the waste portion of the work. Lock the fence at the desired setting and check that the blade is no more than 1/4 inch above the stock. Lock the blade-height setting.

This cut is made in the same way as a rip cut. Turn on the saw. Butt the stock against the fence and guide it forward into the blade (5–38). If the piece is less than five inches wide, use a push stick to make the cut. Guide the workpiece past the blade onto a take-off table or other support stand. Shut off the saw and let it come to a complete stop before retrieving the stock or the cut-off (5–39).

When the stock is narrow, the guard may contact the fence and limit positioning. In the case, follow the procedures described in Ripping Thin and Narrow Stock on pages 77 to 79.

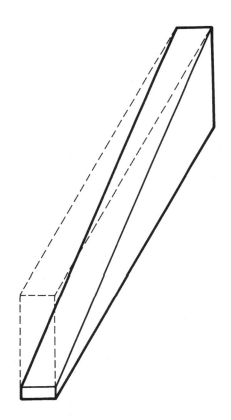

5–36. An edge miter or bevel goes from face to face on a piece of stock at an angle.

5–37. A chamfer goes from the face on a piece of stock to an edge or end at an angle.

CUTTING EDGE MITERS AND CHAMFERS

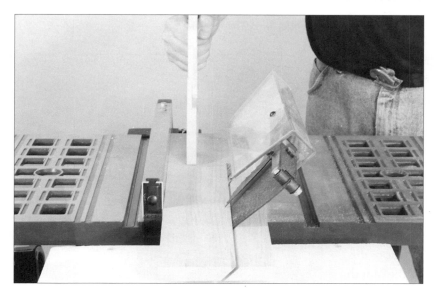

5–38. An edge miter or chamfer cut is made the same way as a rip cut except that the blade is tilted. Stand clear of the kickback zone and keep stock against the table and fence.

5–39. Push the stock completely past the blade onto a take-off table. Shut off the saw and let the blade stop turning before retrieving the cutoff.

COMPOUND MITERS

Compound miters are miters that are usually made by tilting the blade and turning the miter gauge (5–40). They are most commonly used when stock is inclined, as in a cove molding along the ceiling line of a house or when making picture frames.

Refer to Compound-Miter Settings to make the initial setting for the compound miter. Once the setting has been made, make a test cut in scrap wood to make sure it is correct. Make minor adjustments until you are sure the setting is correct.

If the blade tilts toward the left miter slot, the

miter gauge has to be tilted clockwise for right-hand miters (5–41) and counterclockwise for left-hand miters (5–42 and 5–43). The *setting* of the miter gauge will be the same for both right and left miters. The difference is that the miter gauge will be turned the opposite way (5–44).

If the blade tilts toward the right miter-gauge slot, reverse the way the miter gauge is turned for the two cuts; that is, tilt the miter gauge *counterclockwise* for right-hand miters and *clockwise* for left-hand miters.

As mentioned above, make test pieces and check their fit before beginning the actual cuts (5–45). Slight adjustments can improve the fit. Avoid large adjustments; they make it more difficult to achieve a perfect fit. Control the length of the parts being cut by attaching an auxiliary face to the miter gauge and using a stop block.

COMPOUND-MITER SETTINGS	Refer to the following information before cutting compound miters. Using the settings indicated will ensure accurate cuts that may require only some fine-adjustment.	

Incline of Work	Blade/Angle	Miter-Gauge Angle
5°	44¾°	85°
10°	44¼°	80¼°
15°	43¼°	75½°
20°	41¾°	71¼°
25°	40°	67°
30°	37¾°	63½°
35°	35¼°	60½°
40°	32½°	57¼°
45°	30°	54¾°
50°	27°	52½°
55°	24°	50¾°
60°	21°	49°

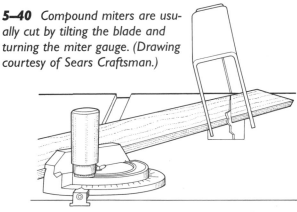

5–40 *Compound miters are usually cut by tilting the blade and turning the miter gauge. (Drawing courtesy of Sears Craftsman.)*

5–41. *Cutting a right-hand compound miter for a picture frame. The auxiliary face on the miter gauge sweeps the scrap away from the blade. Retract the miter gauge and piece after the cut is complete and shut off the saw. Do not retrieve the cut-off until the blade has come to a complete stop.*

5–42. *The miter gauge is turned the opposite way when a miter cut is being made on the left end of the stock. The opposite edge of the stock is against the auxiliary face.*

(continued on following page)

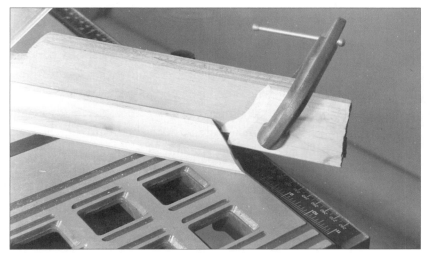

5–43. A stop has been clamped to the auxiliary face to control stock length. The most critical length is where the picture goes; this is in the rabbet. Measure carefully. It is better to have the part slightly long than short.

5–44. The cut is made holding the stock securely against the auxiliary face while advancing the miter gauge. The cutoff is swept away from the blade by the auxiliary face. Retract the miter gauge and workpiece. Shut off the saw. Do not retrieve the cutoff until the blade has come to a complete stop.

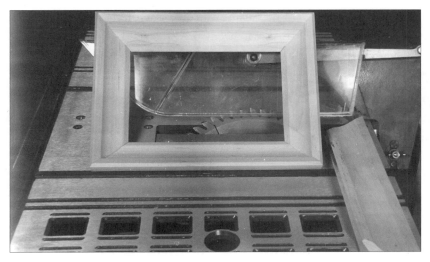

5–45. Making initial cuts to test pieces ensures that the correct settings have been made and reduces waste. The piece on the right was the test stock for this picture frame.

Rabbets

Rabbets are L-shaped channels along stock (5–46). This section presents information on cutting end and edge rabbets with a single blade. Refer to Rabbet Joints on pages 57 and 58 for information on cutting rabbets with a dado head.

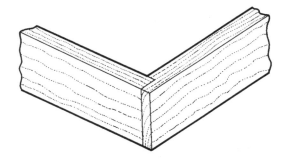

5–46. Rabbets are L-shaped channels along stock. Shown here is an end rabbet.

EDGE RABBETS

Edge rabbets, L-shaped channels along the edge of a piece of stock, require two cuts. The first cut is made with the face of the piece on the table and the edge against the fence. Begin by raising the blade to the depth of the rabbet cut. Lock the elevating handwheel at this setting. The distance between the edge of the blade farthest from the fence and the fence determines the width of the rabbet. Use a tooth that points away from the fence to make this setting. Lock the fence at the desired setting (5–47).

Since this is not a through cut, the splitter must be removed to make the cut. A featherboard may be used for greater workpiece control. Turn on the saw and make the cut into the face of the workpiece (5–48). Use a push stick to guide the work across the blade. Push the piece completely clear of the blade and shut off the saw.

The second cut is made with the stock on edge. Position the piece so that the cutoff will fall free from the fence. If it were trapped between the blade and fence, it could kick back. Readjust the fence and blade height so that the second saw kerf will meet the first. Lock the blade-height and fence settings. A featherboard can be used above or on the infeed side of the blade for greater control (5–49). Do not allow the featherboard to pinch the cutoff against the blade. This would result in a kickback.

Turn on the saw and guide the stock into the blade. Keep the face of the piece against the fence and the edge on the table. Use a push stick to guide the stock across the blade. Push the piece completely clear of the blade and shut off the saw (5–50).

It is also possible to make the edge cut first, if desired. The important thing to remember is to let the cutoff fall free. It should be not trapped between the blade and fence or between the blade and featherboard.

END RABBETS

End rabbets can be cut in a similar fashion as edge rabbets or they can be cut using a series of cuts with the stock in the horizontal plane. When using the two-cut method—the method used when cutting edge rabbets—care must be exercised when the piece is positioned vertically on its end grain. The piece must be controlled with a jig, such as a tenoning jig. Attempting to hold the piece vertically and against the fence will result in a loss of control and possible kickback.

Begin the two-cut end rabbet by setting the distance from a stop block (a true piece of stock about two inches thick, two inches wide, and four inches long) (5–51). The stop block is butted to the fence adjacent to the blade. Once

(text continued on page 93)

CUTTING EDGE RABBETS

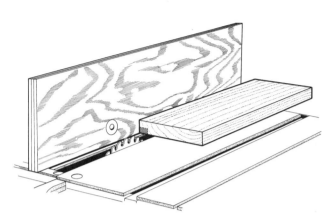

5–47. *Cutting an edge rabbet. Set the blade height and the fence position for the rabbet cut. Lock the settings. It is better to make an error in the waste area; this way, there is a second chance at making an accurate cut.*

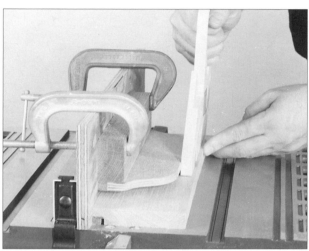

5–48. *A barrier has been positioned over the blade to reduce the chance of contact. The barrier clears the work as it is advanced. Keep the stock against the fence and table.*

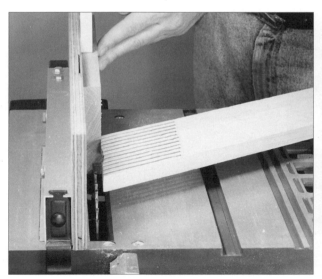

5–49. *The featherboard holds the stock against the fence and acts as a barrier. Make this cut as if it were a rip cut.*

5–50. *Use a push stick to complete the cut. Push the work past the blade, and then shut off the saw. Do not retrieve the cutoff until the blade stops turning. Note how the cutoff fell free. Trapping the cutoff usually results in a kickback.*

END RABBETS WITH TWO CUTS

5–51. Cutting an end rabbet. The stop determines the position of the fence relative to the blade. It also prevents any chance of binding when the cut is made.

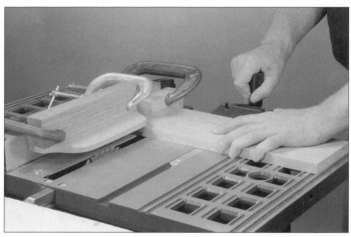

5–52. The stop is clamped to the fence and the work is butted to the stop. Make the cut as if it were a crosscut. Notice the barrier guard clamped to the fence. This will reduce the chance of operator contact with the blade.

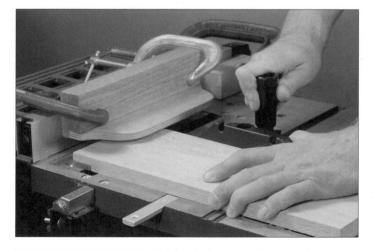

5–53. Complete the first cut, and then shut off the saw.

END RABBETS WITH TWO CUTS

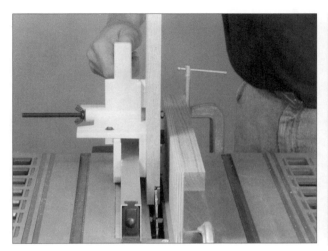

5–54. Once the jig is positioned so that the blade lines up correctly, the cut can be made. It is best to have the blade too low rather than too high. This provides a second chance of making an accurate cut. Notice the barrier clamped to the table. It reduces the chance of contact with the blade.

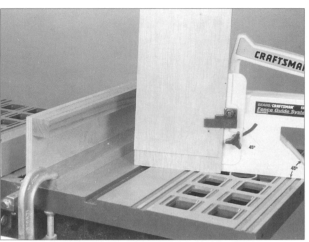

5–55. The cuts line up correctly. The rabbeted piece can be removed from the jig.

the distance is set, the fence is clamped in place. The stop block is then clamped to the fence at the infeed end near where the operator stands. Adjust the blade height to the rabbet depth and lock the blade-elevating handwheel.

Place the edge of the workpiece against the miter gauge and butt the end to the stop block, which should be clamped to the fence (5–52). Turn on the saw and make a cut into the face of the workpiece (5–53). Shut off the saw after completing the cut.

The mating cut is made using a tenoning jig. The jig holds the piece vertically and guides it into the blade. It is positioned in the miter-gauge slot while other jigs ride on the fence. The workpiece is clamped to the tenoning jig with the piece's end grain on the table. Adjust the position of the stock until the cutting line is aligned with

the blade. This is done by moving the fence or by moving the base of the tenoning jig into position.

Secure the base once it is positioned.

Turn on the saw and guide the tenoning jig into the saw blade. Keep your hands on the jig and clear of the blade (5–54). Once the cut is completed, shut off the saw and allow the blade to come to a complete stop. Remove the work from the tenoning jig (5–55).

When making a rabbet cut with a series of cuts, the setup is the same as it is for the first cut of the two-cut end rabbet. Make the first cut as described above (5–56) and then move the stock ⅛ inch away from the stop block and make another cut (5–57). Continue this process until the rabbet is formed (5–58 and 5–59).

END RABBETS WITH A SERIES OF CUTS

5–56. When a series of cuts are being made, the setup is the same as used for cutting an end rabbet with two cuts. The only difference is that the blade height must be exact. Shown here is the first cut.

5–57. After the first cut is made, the stock is moved about ⅛ inch away from the stop and the second cut is made.

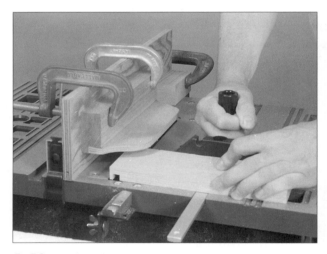

5–58. The process of moving the stock away from the stop is continued until the rabbet is formed.

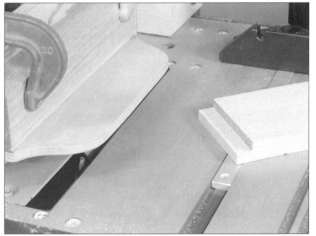

5–59. The completed end rabbet resembles the two-cut rabbet, except that the bottom is usually not as smooth.

Dadoes

Dadoes are U-shaped channels made in wood. This section contains information on making lazy and dovetail dadoes with a single blade.

Refer to Common Dadoes on pages 54 to 57 for information on cutting dadoes with a dado head.

LAZY DADOES

The procedure for cutting a lazy dado (5–60) is similar to that for making a rabbet with a series of saw cuts. For cross-grain dadoes, set the stop block on the fence to the near side of the blade in order to make the first cut (5–61). Position the fence so the blade will cut on the dado side

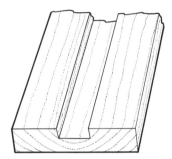

5–60. Lazy dado.

of the layout line nearest to the fence. Lock the fence setting and move the stop block back to the infeed end of the fence and clamp it securely to the fence. Set the blade height to the depth of the dado. Position the end of the workpiece on the stop block, with the workpiece's edge against the miter gauge and the face to be dadoed on the table. Turn on the saw and make the cut (5–62). When all parts have been cut, shut off the saw and allow the blade to come to a complete stop.

Next, adjust the stop block and fence so that the blade cuts into the dado side of the layout line farthest from the fence (5–63). Reposition the stop block at the infeed end of the fence and make the cut the same way as the first cut was made.

Complete the dado with a series of cuts, moving one saw kerf away from the stop block for the next cut. Continue moving away from the stop block for additional cuts (5–64). When the dado has been completed, test its fit to the mating part. Make any necessary adjustments (5–65).

5–61. Cutting a lazy dado. A cross-grain lazy dado is cut much like a rabbet. Begin by setting the blade height and adjusting the fence to the shoulder that is closer to the fence. Put the blade in the waste area.

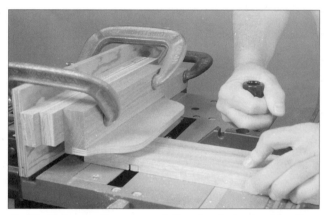

5–62. Make the first cut to define the dado shoulder. Butt the stock to the stop, and make this cut the same way a crosscut is made.

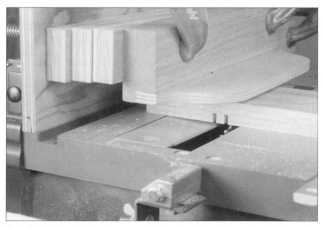

5–63. Repeat the process to make the other shoulder cut.

(continued on following page)

CROSS-GRAIN LAZY DADOES *(CONTINUED)*

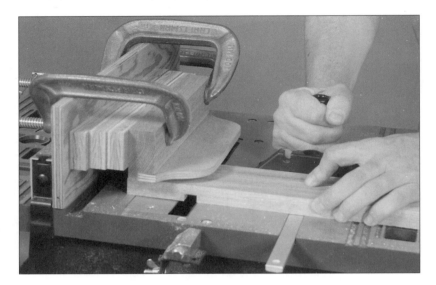

5–64. *Make a series of cuts, moving away from the stop. Continue this process until the other cut is reach.*

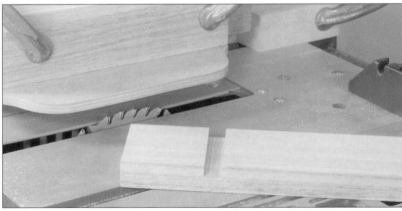

5–65. *The completed dado. Test the fit of the dado with the mating piece. Make any necessary adjustments.*

When cutting a lazy dado with the grain, position the edge of the workpiece against the fence and move the fence until the saw blade lines up with the layout line that is closer to the fence (5–66). Make sure the saw kerf will be cut in the dado area. Secure the fence and adjust the blade height to the dado depth. For additional control, featherboards could be added to hold the stock against the fence or table.

Position the stock against the fence and clear of the saw blade. Turn on the saw and guide the stock along the fence into the saw blade. Use a push stick to complete the cut. When all parts have been cut, readjust the fence for the line farther from the fence (5–67). Make sure that the saw kerf is cut in the area to be dadoed. Repeat the process of cutting the kerf for the opposite edge of the dado. When all parts have been cut, move the fence over one saw kerf (5–68). Lock the fence and make another cut. Continue this process until the dado is complete (5–69).

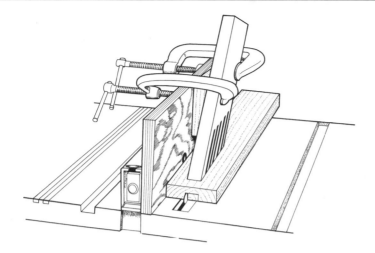

5–66. Cutting a lazy dado with the grain. Shown here is the setup. Move the fence until the blade lines up with the shoulder layout line that is closer to the fence. Then set the blade height for the depth of the dado. The featherboard acts as a barrier and hold-down.

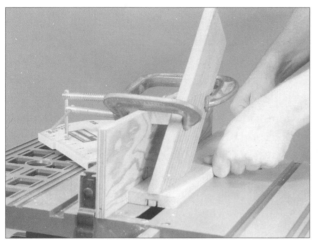

5–67. Readjust the fence for the shoulder that is farther from the fence. Make this cut in all parts.

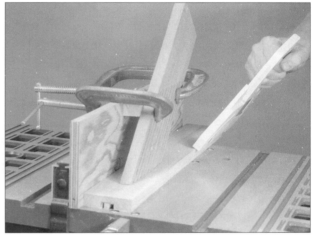

5–68. Move the fence 1/8 inch closer to the fence for another cut. Continue this process until the first cut is met.

5–69. The completed dado will look like this. Check its fit with the mating part.

Dovetail Dadoes

The dovetail dado is a lazy dado that is often used to attach a drawer front to the drawer sides (5–70). The methods used to cut lazy dadoes described on pages 95 to 97 can be adapted when cutting dovetail dadoes. This joint works best when the drawer side or mating part is held at least ½ inch in from the end of the drawer front. The widest part of the dado is equal to the thickness of the drawer side, usually ½ inch.

Lay out the dovetail positions on the edge of the drawer front. The taper for a ½-inch-deep dado should be from 5/16 to ½ inch. Tilt the blade to the incline of the dovetailed dado sides and cut the sides of the dado. This will require two separate cuts. One cut will be made using the left miter-gauge slot (5–71), and the other will be made using the right miter-gauge slot (5–72). When these cuts are complete, there may be some material in the bottom of the dado that will have to be removed with a chisel. Make the cuts at the bench and prepare the ½-inch drawer stock for machining.

First, make the cuts on the two faces of the drawer sides, and then cut the inclined sides of the end. Set the distance from the fence to the edge of the blade farthest from the fence to the depth of the dovetail dado (½ inch). Cut both faces of the end. The stock thickness at the bottom of the kerfs should be equal to the narrowest end of the dovetail dado (½ to 5/16 inch).

Now tilt the saw blade to the same angle that was used on the edges of the dado. Use a tenoning jig to control the stock for the end-grain cut. No material is removed from the end of the piece (5–73). The inclined cut tilts back from the end where no stock is removed. Make the cut on both faces (5–74 and 5–75). Check the fit of the mating parts (5–76). They should slide together easily. If the fit is too tight, remove a little more stock from both faces. Remember, since stock is being removed from both faces, the adjustment that is made should be one-half the difference between the two parts. For example, if the part is 1/32 inch oversize, move the fence 1/64 inch (½ of the interference).

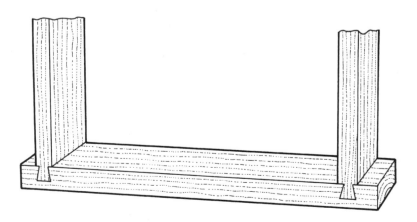

5–70. The dovetail dado is an excellent drawer joint.

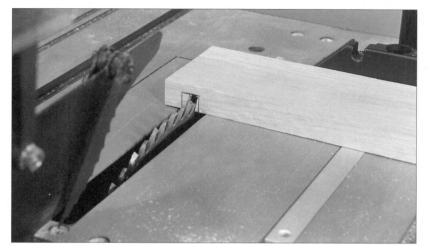

5–71. The first incline is cut using the miter gauge in the left miter-gauge slot.

5–72. The second incline is cut using the miter gauge in the right miter-gauge slot. Once the two sides are cut, the middle can be sawn out in the lazy dado fashion described on pages 95 to 97.

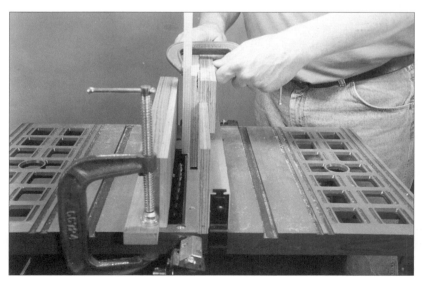

5–73. When the end grain is being cut, the setup includes a jig that is positioned over the fence to hold the pieces vertically for cutting. These cuts should never be made without some type of jig. The blade height and angle for cutting these drawer sides are the same as for the drawer front. The fence is positioned so that the blade does not change the stock thickness at the end of the piece. A barrier guard has been positioned to prevent contact with the blade.

(continued on following page)

5–74. The inclined cut forms one-half of the dovetail. The piece is reversed and cut again, to complete the dovetail.

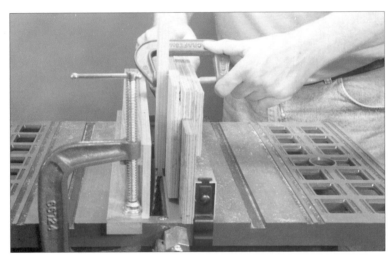

5–75. No adjustments are required for the mating cut. The dovetail is complete when the cut is made.

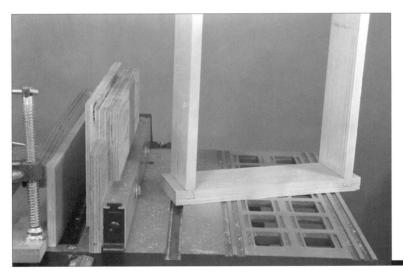

5–76. Test the fit of the pieces. The pieces should not have to be forced together. This joint is precise, but quick to make. Practice on scrap to master it.

Lap Joints

A lap joint is a two-part joint in which both parts are identical. It is used wherever two pieces of stock cross or lap over each other. When a blade instead of a dado head is being used to make a lap joint, two cuts are required on both parts. These cuts are called the shoulder and the cheek cuts. The shoulder cut is made first.

The shoulder cut is made across the grain at a depth of one-half the stock thickness. It is made at a distance from the end of the piece that is equal to the width of the stock that fits in the lap. Make sure the saw kerf is kept in the waste area of the stock. The cut is made in the same way as an end rabbet; the miter gauge and a stop are used to position the stock (5–77).

The mating cheek cut is made using a tenoning or universal jig (5–78). The jig clamps the piece in the vertical position Once the piece is clamped in the tenoning jig, the jig is positioned relative to the blade. Keep the blade in the waste

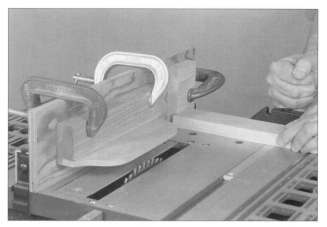

5–77. Cutting lap joints. The shoulder cut is made using a stop and a barrier. The blade height is one-half the stock's thickness. The distance from the end of the piece to the far side of the kerf is equal to the stock's width (or 1/32 inch more, to allow for cleanup).

section of the stock. Adjust the blade height to the shoulder cut. It should be high enough to meet the middle of the kerf. Lock all settings. Make sure the cut-off is not pinched and can fall free when the cut is made.

Make the cheek cut by turning on the saw with

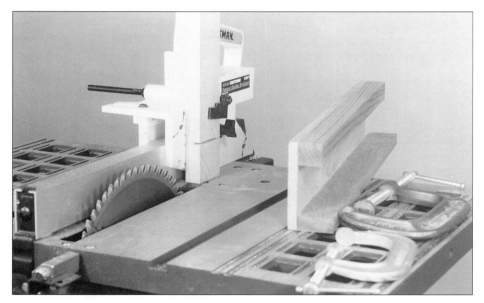

5–78. A tenoning or universal jig is used to control stock in the vertical position. Never try to make this cut without a jig to control the stock. For safety, a barrier should also be installed.

the tenoning jig and workpiece both clear of the blade. Guide the tenoning jig into the blade. Keep both hands clear of the blade while guiding the workpiece into the blade (5–79). When the cut is complete, retract the jig and turn off the power (5–80). Let the blade come to a complete stop before releasing the workpiece from the jig. Test the fit between the parts and make any needed adjustments (5–81).

Refer to Lap Joints and Tenons on pages 58 to 61 for information on making lap joints with a dado head. Also refer to Making a Frame with Lap Joints on pages 119 to 121 for information on making a door frame with lap joints.

5–81. Test the fit between the parts, and then make any needed adjustments.

Tenons

A tenon is one part of the two-part mortise-and-tenon-joint (5–82). The tenon is similar to a lap joint except that there are two cheek and shoulder cuts instead of one.

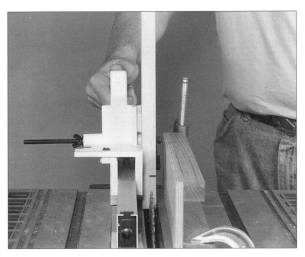

5–79. The blade should line up with the shoulder cut. Turn on the saw and guide the tenoning jig forward. This is a heavy rip cut, so do not force the work.

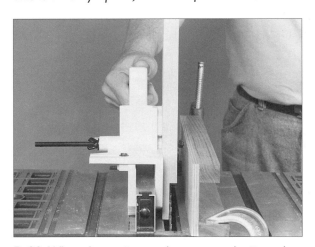

5–80. When the cut is complete, retract the jig and shut off the saw.

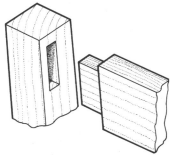

5–82. The tenon is the horizontally positioned part of this two-part joint known as a mortise-and-tenon joint. The information in this section describes cutting a tenon for the through-mortise-and-tenon joint.

The first two cuts are the shoulder cuts. The depth of the shoulder cut is approximately one-third the thickness of the workpiece. The distance from the end of the piece varies according to the type of mortise-and-tenon joint. The through mortise-and-tenon joint requires a tenon equal in length to the width of the mating piece (5–83). All other tenons are shorter than the through tenon. Use a stop attached to the fence or table in order to position stock for the shoulder cuts (5–84 to 5–86).

The cheek cuts are made using a tenoning jig (5–87). Adjust the tenoning jig so that the blade cuts a kerf that meets the shoulder. Keep the kerf in the waste portion of the cheek. Make sure that the stock cut away during the cheek cut is not pinched and will fall free when the cut is made. Turn on the saw and guide the tenoning jig into

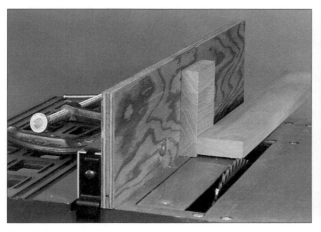

5–83. The tenon in a through-mortise-and-tenon joint requires a length equal to the width of the mating piece. Both parts of this joint are of equal width. Refer to Through Mortises on pages 61 and 62 for information on cutting the through mortise.

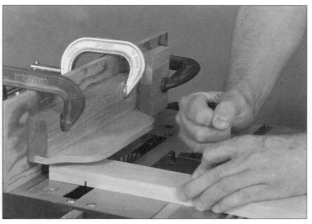

5–85. The first shoulder is formed. The piece must be turned over for a mating cut. The barrier makes the job safer.

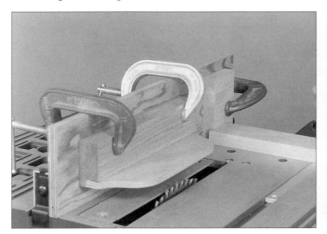

5–84. Position the end against the stop for both shoulder cuts. The blade height is about one-third of the stock's thickness.

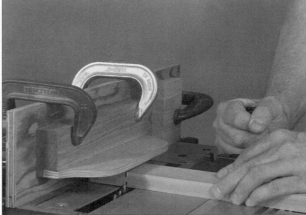

5–86. The second shoulder is cut. It lines up with its mate. Once all shoulder cuts are made, the cheek cut can be made.

the blade (5–88). Keep both hands on the jig and away from the blade. When the cut is complete, retract the jig and turn off the power. Let the blade come to a complete stop before releasing the stock from the jig and making the second cut (5–89).

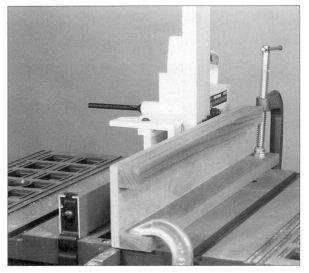

5–87. *The tenoning jig holds the piece vertically for the cheek cut. This is a heavy rip cut, so do not force the saw. The barrier has been positioned to make the cut safer.*

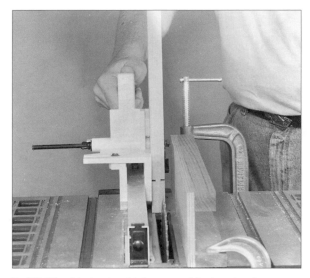

5–88. *The blade should line up with the cheek cut. Turn on the saw and make the cut.*

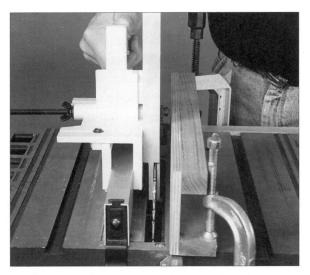

5–89. *A second cut is required to complete the tenon. Reverse the piece and make the cut.*

Refer to Lap Joints and Tenons on pages 58 to 61 for information on making tenons with a dado head.

Through Mortises

A through, or open, mortise (5–90) is the mating piece to the tenon cut described in the previous section, Tenons. To make this mortise, use

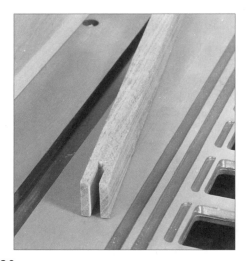

5–90. *A through mortise is the mate to the tenon cut described in the previous section.*

the tenon to lay it out. Clamp the workpiece in the tenoning jig and use the layout line to position the stock. The blade should be in the section where the tenon will be located (5–91).

5–91. *Cutting a through mortise. Position the blade in the tenon area. This will orient it correctly so that the through mortise can be cut.*

5–92. *The through mortise is cut in the same way as a tenon. The only difference is the position of the blade.*

The first cut is similar to the cheek cut made on the tenon, except that no shoulder cut is required. When the mortise is centered on the piece, the piece can be reversed in the tenoning jig and a second cut can be made. This cut establishes the outer edges of the mortise. Any stock remaining between the cheeks of the mortise can be removed by repositioning the tenoning jig.

Make the cuts in the same way as those described in the previous section, Tenons. Remember, hands should be kept on the tenoning jig and away from the blade (5–92). Let the blade come to a complete stop before adjusting the tenoning jig or reversing the workpiece (5–93). Check the fit between the two parts and make any needed adjustments. The pieces should slide together without force (5–94). This way, there will be room for glue. A forced fit is too tight.

Refer to Making Through Mortises on pages

5–93. *The workpiece is reversed and a second cut is made. If the pieces do not fit together properly because of excess wood on the workpiece, the tenoning jig will have to be set a second time.*

5–94. *Test the fit of the mortise and tenon. The parts should slide together with no resistance.*

61 and 62 for information on making through mortises with a dado head.

Cove Cuts

A cove (5–95) is a curved recess cut into a piece of stock. Most coved profiles can be cut using a blade and an inclined fence. Coves are used for restoration work, pencil drawers, and furniture parts.

Begin by laying out the cove on the end of the workpiece. Determine the arc and then draw it on

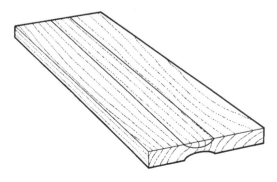

5–95. *A cove is a curved recess in a piece of stock.*

the end. Remove most of the wood in the cove using rip cuts (5–96). For large areas and production work, a dado head may also be used. Adjust the fence and blade or dado height for each cut and try to leave a minimum of stock in the coved area.

For accurate layout of the cove, make a parallel guide like that shown in 5–97 and 5–98. Use

5–96. *Cutting a cove. Use rip cuts to remove most of the stock in the cove. Adjust the fence position and blade height to accomplish this.*

1¼-inch-thick stock for the parts. Hold the four parts together with ¼-inch #20 T-nuts and bolts. The parallel guide will help produce the correct setting the first time.

Select the appropriate blade for cove-cutting. For shallow, wide coves, a 10-inch-diameter blade works well. For deep, circular-shaped coves, an 8-inch-diameter blade works well. Make sure the blade selected has fine teeth. This means, that if a carbide-tipped blade is being used, it should have 40 or more teeth, and if a tool-steel blade is being used, it should be a fine paneling blade. This will reduce the amount of sanding required.

Adjust the blade height to the deepest portion

5–97. A user-made parallel guide should be utilized to lay out the cove. It will make the job easier. Set the parallel pieces on the guide to the width of the cove.

of the cove (5–99). Set the parallel guide to the cove width and tighten the bolts to hold the setting. Place the parallel guide over the blade and turn the guide so that one tooth of the blade touches each edge of the two parallel pieces of the guide.

The parallel guide should now be resting at an angle to the blade (5–100). This angle is the angle at which the fence must be adjusted for cove-cutting. Copy this angle with a sliding T-bevel. Select a stiff, true piece of stock to use as the auxiliary fence. Set the fence to the angle of the sliding T-bevel. Make sure the fence is between the front of the saw and the blade. This allows the thrust of the blade to force the work against the fence.

Adjust the fence with reference to the stock being cut (5–101). The edge of the cove should just touch a tooth that points toward the fence. Clamp the fence securely in place. Make sure the

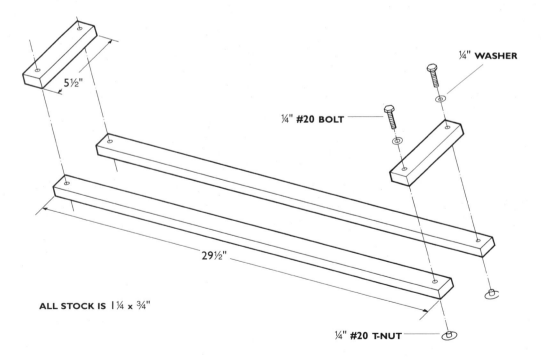

5–98. An exploded drawing of the parallel guide. Use the information provided here to make your own guide.

5–99. *Set the blade height to the cove depth.*

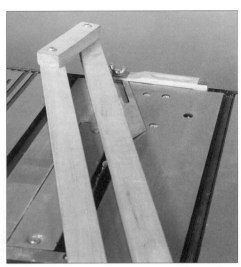

5–100. *Using the parallel guide to determine the angle of the fence. One tooth of the blade touches each edge of the parallel parts of the guide on the table. Copy the angle with a sliding T-bevel.*

5–101. *Position the auxiliary fence with reference to the piece being coved. The blade should line up with the cove.*

5–102. *Lower the blade and position featherboards to control the workpiece.*

clamps are not in the path of the workpiece along the control edge of the fence.

Lower the blade (5–102). About ⅛ inch of the blade should be above the table for the first cut.

Light cuts produce the best results. Clamp two featherboards to the table. These will hold the stock against the fence. Mark the fence side of the stock to avoid reversing the pieces between

5–103. Take a light cut. Do not force the work. Resistance can mean that the cut is too deep. Forcing the stock could result in a kickback.

cuts. This is very important if the cove is not centered. Put the mark on the side that is not cut.

Turn on the saw and guide the piece across the blade (5–103). The piece should be held firmly against the inclined fence. Push sticks should be used to keep hands clear of the blade and improve control of the stock. *Note:* If there is feeding resistance, the blade may be too high. Lower the blade and try again.

After all the parts have been cut, raise the blade about 1/16 inch. Make the second cut in all the parts. Repeat this process until the layout line is reached. Remember, as the blade is raised, more

5–104. When approaching the layout line, take lighter cuts. This will reduce the amount of sanding needed.

teeth come in contact with the work. This means the blade has to work harder and is more likely to kick back. As the cove gets deeper, take lighter cuts–about 1/32 inch.

When approaching the layout line, take lighter cuts (5–104). This will reduce the amount of sanding needed. Feed the stock slowly on the final pass to make it smoother. Sometimes two passes at the final setting make the cove smoother. Sand the cove to the desired smoothness.

Resawing

Resawing is the process of ripping a thick piece of stock into two thinner pieces. Resawn pieces are often glued together to make panels for cabinet sides or doors. The grain is often matched at the glue line to give a book-like effect. This is commonly known as a book-match (5–105).

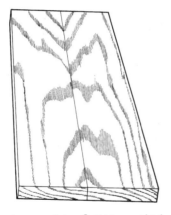

5–105. Resawing consists of ripping a thick piece of stock into two thinner ones. Resawn pieces are often glued together to make attractive panels for door or cabinet sides, as shown here. This board is said to be book-matched; that is, the grain of the two pieces matches at the glue line.

Stock that will be resawn should be true. Its edges and faces should be parallel. There should be no knots or other defects.

Select a blade appropriate for heavy rip cuts. A 10-inch-diameter blade with 8 to 24 teeth should be appropriate. A coarse blade will ensure faster feeding and less chance of binding or kickback. Since the guard cannot be used for this operation, a special C-shaped bracket must be made. Two pieces of stock are needed to make this barrier. The first should be 3/4 inch thick and as wide and long as the fence (5–106). It is attached to another piece of stock 3/4 inch thick, about six to eight inches wide, and as long as the fence. Use glue and screws or nails to make the joint strong.

5–106. This barrier is user-made and will keep the operator's hands away from the blade. It should be slightly longer than the table.

The stock that will be resawn must be thick enough to yield two pieces of desired thickness. For example, a 3/4-inch-thick piece cannot be resawn into two pieces 3/8 inch thick. This is because the kerf will take up a thickness of 1/8 inch or more. A 3/4-inch-thick piece will produce two pieces that are 1/4 inch thick while allowing for a kerf and sanding or planing of the sawn surface.

Set the distance from the fence to the blade at the desired stock thickness, plus ⅟16 to ⅛ inch more for sanding or planing the stock (5–107). Lower the blade beneath the table and position the stock that will be resawn next to the fence. Move the special bracket toward the workpiece.

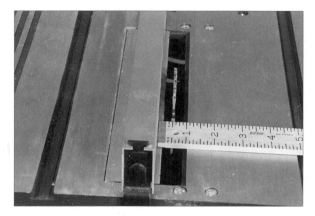

5–107. *Set the distance from the blade to the fence at the desired thickness. Remember to allow an extra ⅟16 to ⅛ inch for planing and sanding. Lock the fence at the desired setting.*

There should be ⅛ inch between the workpiece and the side of the bracket that is the same size as the fence. The other leg of the bracket should be clamped to the saw so that it cannot move. This bracket will make access to the blade more difficult because it acts as a barrier.

Set the blade height as slightly less than one-half the stock thickness or no more than one inch. With the edge of the workpiece on the table, its face against the fence, and its end clear of the blade, turn on the saw. Make a rip cut through the piece (5–108). Use a push stick to control the workpiece. Place the edge of the workpiece on the table, the same edge against the fence, and make a second rip cut into the opposite edge.

On a narrow workpiece, there will be a thin strip of wood holding the two sides together. In most cases, the pieces will split apart easily. They can then be glued together and sanded or planed. On wider stock, the blade will have to be

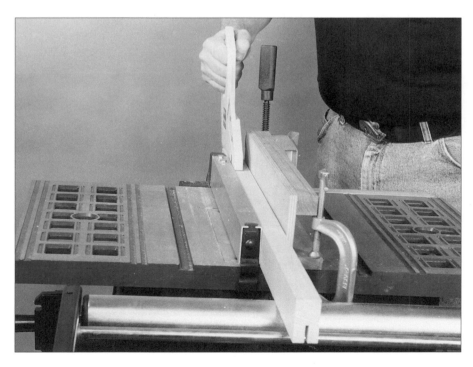

5–108. *The blade is set at one inch above the table. The rip cut is made in the normal way. The roller stand, shown in the foreground, supports the work as it leaves the table.*

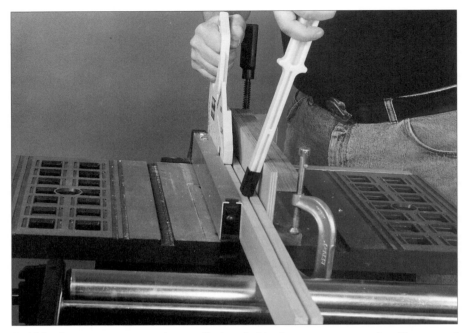

5–109. *Continue cutting until a small piece holds the two parts together. The second push stick provides greater control over the work.*

raised another inch or to slightly less than one-half the stock width. Make another rip cut from the edge (5–109). Be sure to keep the same face of the workpiece against the fence. Separate these pieces when a thin strip of wood remains (5–110).

The blade is set at a one-inch height to reduce the load on the blade and motor. This, in turn, will reduce the chance of a kickback. The stock hardness and the horsepower of the saw may allow a slightly higher (or lower) setting. Experience will indicate the correct setting for the saw. Avoid using blades with a large number of teeth. They will slow the feed speed and cause burning. They can also contribute to kickback.

5–110. *The pieces can be separated using a chisel or hand pressure and then glued together to form a panel, if desired.*

CHAPTER **6** **Cutting Plastic Laminates**

Plastic laminates are made by bonding kraft paper and plastic resin under heat and pressure. They serve as decorative and protective covers on sheet stock, and are used on kitchen countertops, bars, and bathroom vanities.

Plastic-laminate sheets are similar to sheet stock in length and width. They are available in widths from 24 to 60 inches and in lengths from 60 to 120 inches. However, plastic laminates are thinner than sheet stock (about 1/16 inch thick), and are very flexible and more difficult to control. This material has a tendency to slip under the fence (6–1).

There are three stages to working with plastic laminates: cutting, gluing, and trimming. The information that follows presents guidelines on cutting plastic laminates with a table saw and then information on bonding and trimming this material.

6–1. Plastic laminates, which are only about 1/16 inch thick, can slip under the fence. An auxiliary fence, as shown in 6–3, can eliminate this problem.

CUTTING TECHNIQUES   Follow these procedures when cutting plastic laminates:

❶ Be aware of grain or pattern direction. It may be necessary to plan cuts according to the pattern so that joints match up correctly.

❷ Select a triple-chip, 60- to-80-tooth carbide-tipped blade for best results (6–2). This type of blade will resist wear and produce the best cut.

6–2. The triple-chip carbide-tipped blade works well on plastic laminates. Use a blade with 60 to 80 teeth.

❸ Attach a wooden auxiliary fence to the fence, to prevent the laminate from creeping under it. To prevent the laminate from lifting as it goes over the blade, also use a featherboard (6–3). Feed the laminate slowly into the blade, good-side up.

6–3. Use an auxiliary fence and featherboard when cutting plastic laminates, to increase control over the work-piece.

(continued on following page)

❹ Cut the laminate one-half to one inch oversize. This is to allow for slight error and for trimming. Wear eye protection when making the cut. ,

❺ A common practice in laminate shops when long pieces are being cut and there is no helper is to use a wooden countertop as a support for the plastic laminate at the front of the saw (6–4). The countertop is positioned at the front of the saw on sawhorses. The laminate is laid on the countertop good-face up and then guided across the countertop and saw table into the blade. Then the triple-chip blade is used to cut the laminate. The laminate is also cut with its good-face up.

6-4. An unfinished countertop, positioned in front of the table saw, is being used to support the laminate. Long or wide pieces may be difficult to control. Either use a support such as the countertop or have someone help you. It will save material and make the job safer.

❻ When cutting plastic laminate the long way, concentrate on keeping the laminate edge against the fence. It may be necessary to apply tape to the anti-kickback pawls so they will not scratch the laminate.

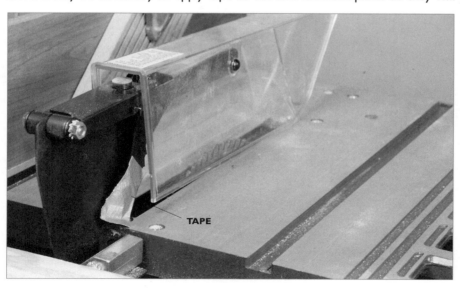

TAPE

6–5. Tape is sometimes applied to the anti-kick-back pawls to prevent them from scratching the face of the plastic laminate. Be sure to remove the tape when the plastic laminates have all been cut.

Bonding Techniques

After the plastic laminate is cut, it is bonded to the sheet stock. The most common adhesive used for the bonding is contact adhesive. This type of glue requires no clamping pressure. The bond occurs when the dry rubber adhesive on one surface comes into contact with the dry rubber adhesive on the other surface. Polyvinyl acetate and urea-formaldehyde are the most effective glues in terms of strength and resistance to heat and cold, but their use is not practical because of the pressure required during clamping and the time required for the adhesive to cure.

Apply the contact cement to the front and back edges and to both ends of the sheet stock, using a brush or roller. Let the contact cement dry. Test its dryness with a piece of brown paper. If it does not stick, the surfaces are ready.

Place the ends of the sheet stock and the plastic laminate in position. Be sure to align them correctly *before* bonding them. Once the surfaces touch, they cannot be moved. Then align the front and back surfaces.

Trim the front, back, and ends so that the tops of the plastic laminate and sheet stock can be glued in position. (See the following section on trimming plastic laminates.) Now apply the contact cement to the top of the sheet stock and the top laminate. After the cement dries, align the two surfaces. To prevent the tops from sticking before they are aligned, place sticks between the laminate and sheet stock.

Trimming Techniques

Plastic laminates can be trimmed with a router, laminate trimmer, or hand scraper. A laminate trimmer is a specialized power tool designed for laminate work. It is lighter than a router and easier to work in corners. It uses a bit that will cut straight or at an angle when the base is raised or lowered.

A laminate-trimming bit or panel bit can be used with the router. The laminate-trimming bit works better because it has a ball-bearing pilot tip.

The hand scraper removes small amounts of stock, leaving the plastic laminate very smooth. Scrapers and files are often used to break sharp corners.

7 Door-Making Techniques

Design Factors

The information in this chapter pertains to the construction of frame-and-panel doors. A frame-and-panel door consists of five parts (7–1). The frame has two horizontal parts—the rails—and two vertical parts—the stiles. The rails and stiles are held together with various types of joinery to make the frame. The panel is then held in the frame, usually in a groove or a rabbeted area. The panel may be held in place with molding or it may be trapped in place inside a continuous groove.

The panel is usually made of plywood, solid wood, or raised-panel solid wood, but other materials are sometimes chosen. Cane, corkboard, mirrors, or glass are often used for a specific purpose. If using glass for the panel, make sure that it can be easily replaced.

The frame stock is usually ¾ inch thick and

7–1. *A door consists of two rails, two stiles, and a panel. The stiles are the vertical frame parts and the rails are the horizontal frame parts.*

a minimum of two inches wide. Its length depends on the size of the door. It can be wider than two inches, but if it is narrower, it cannot be rabbeted on both edges and still support a ⅜-inch offset hinge. Stock less than two inches wide does not provide adequate holding strength for most joinery.

Frame-and-panel doors can be one of three types: flush, lip, or overlay (7–2). A flush door sits inside the opening. Its front surface is actually flush with the frame. Lip or rabbeted doors have a ⅜ x ⅜-inch rabbet on the frame. The rabbet fits inside the door opening. The door actually extends ⅜ inch beyond the opening. Overlay doors are larger than their opening.

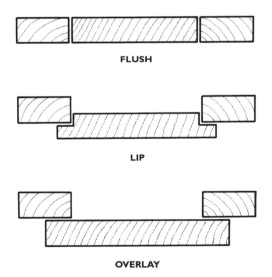

FLUSH

LIP

OVERLAY

7–2. The three most common types of door are flush, lip, and overlay. Flush doors sit inside the door opening. Lip or rabbeted doors have a rabbet on the frame that fits inside the door opening. Overlay doors are larger than their opening.

They cover the opening and extend ¾ inch beyond it.

There are two considerations when determining which type of frame-and-panel door to build: difficulty in conforming the door to the door's opening, and the door's appearance. All doors are joined in the same manner, so as relates to the joinery, they all have the same level of difficulty. However, conforming the door to the opening is more difficult, depending on the type of door being built. Flush doors are the most difficult. That is because the door must fit *inside* the opening. If the door and/or the opening are out of square, then the fit becomes quite difficult. A ⅜-inch-lip door and an overlay door cover the opening and do not have to be precisely square with it.

Appearance considerations often control the decision as to what type of door to use. On smaller projects, overlay doors look too large; they protrude from the front of the cabinet face frame and look oversized. Similarly, on very large cabinets it is difficult to hinge large flush doors and they appear small and undersized.

Before deciding on a type of door, look at some cabinetry to get a feel of what looks right. If you are making a large run of doors, make a couple of experimental doors first. This will help in the decision process and reduce material waste.

Door Size

Door size is determined by the size of the door opening and the type of door being made. Always measure the door opening carefully. Measure it in two or more places. Use a square to check the corners of the opening. If the opening is not square, some allowances will have to be made.

Once the height and width of the opening have been measured, the door size can be determined. If flush doors are being made, subtract

⅛ inch from the height and width of the opening to determine the size of the door. Flush doors are made ⅛ inch shorter and narrower, because the door requires clearance in the opening. A clearance of less than ⅛ inch would mean trouble. When a finish is added to the edges of the door, the door would barely fit.

If ⅜-inch-lip doors are being made, add ½ inch to the height and width of the door opening. Adding ½ inch may seem incorrect considering that a ⅜-inch rabbet will be cut, but this difference of ⅛ inch allows for a space between the door opening and rabbet. This space will allow minor adjustments of the door and will accommodate the hinges. If the door were made any larger, it would have to be put into the opening with a hammer.

If overlay doors are being made, add one inch to the height and width of the opening.

Making a Frame with Lap Joints

After the size of the door has been determined, the next step is to make up a bill of materials. This is a list of all the parts needed to build the project. It includes the parts' dimensions (thickness, width, and length). A bill of materials helps in stock selection and in table-saw setup. In this particular case, since the lap joint goes from end to end, the rails will be as long as the door is wide, and the stiles will be as long as the door is high.

Rip and crosscut the frame parts to size. Lay out the parts, making an X on the material to be removed (7–3). Since the door stiles always go from top to bottom, put the X on the back of the *stiles*. The X goes on the front or exposed face of the *rails*.

Review Setting Up a Dado Head on pages 50 and 51 and Lap Joints and Tenons on pages

FRAME WITH LAP JOINTS

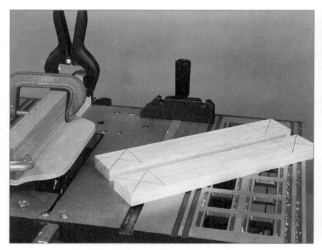

7–3. Put an X on the material that has to be removed. Rails have materials removed from their good face; stiles have material removed from their back face.

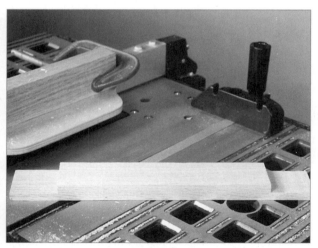

7–4. Check the lap joint for tear-out and to make sure it fits. If the lap joint looks good, all door parts can be cut with one setup.

(continued on following page)

FRAME WITH LAP JOINTS (CONTINUED)

7–5. To cut all the joints, use the method of cutting lap joints described in the section Lap Joints and Tenons on pages 58 to 61. Be sure to have the piece marked with an X facing the table.

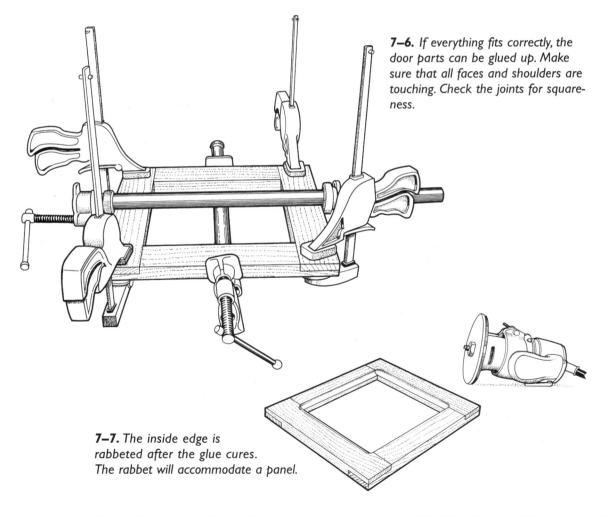

7–6. If everything fits correctly, the door parts can be glued up. Make sure that all faces and shoulders are touching. Check the joints for squareness.

7–7. The inside edge is rabbeted after the glue cures. The rabbet will accommodate a panel.

58 to 61 to set up the dado head and cut a lap joint (7–4). Test the setup to be sure the fit is correct. Proceed to cut all the corners; this set up is correct for all the parts (7–5). Once all parts have been cut, dry-fit them and check the results.

If satisfied with the assembly of the parts, glue them up (7–6). Bar clamps will pull the parts shoulder to shoulder and C-clamps will pull the parts face to face. Be sure to wet the wood with glue, using a brush or applicator; this will improve adhesion. Also put small wooden pads under the clamp jaws to protect the exposed faces of the parts.

After the glue has cured, the clamps can be removed. If a ⅜-inch-lip door is being made, cut a ⅜-by-⅜-inch rabbet into the back face using either a table saw and dado head or a router. Refer to Rabbet Joints on pages 57 and 58 to learn how to cut rabbet joints with a dado head. To accommodate a panel, the inside edge of the frame has to be routed using a ⅜-inch rabbeting bit (7–7). Clamp the stock and rout the rabbet. Be sure to wear protective glasses.

The depth of the rabbet is determined by the thickness of the panel to be installed. The rounded corners made by the router bit will need to be squared up. Use a chisel to square them. Work carefully; do not force the chisel. Light cuts reduce tearing. Use standard clips to hold the panel. These clips are available in the hardware section of most woodworking supply catalogs.

Making a Frame with Haunched Mortise-and-Tenon Joints

The haunched mortise-and-tenon joint (7–8) is used in conjunction with a groove around the inside edge of the door frame. The haunch on the mortise fills the groove at the ends of the door. The haunched mortise-and-tenon joint is most commonly used with wooden door panels. It is not appropriate for glass. If glass panels are being used, lap joints or through mortise-and-tenon joints are a better choice.

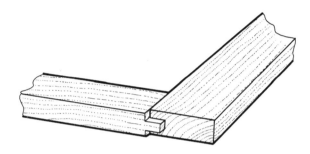

7–8. The haunched mortise-and-tenon joint is used for doors with a wooden panel in the center. The haunch on the mortise fills the groove on the mating piece.

Begin by ripping and crosscutting the frame parts to size. The stiles are as long as the door is tall. The rails are exactly one inch shorter than the door is wide. Lay out the parts and determine the exposed faces. Mark which edge the groove will be cut into (7–9).

The groove should be centered on the edge of the door. It should be about ¼ inch wide and ⅜ inch deep. More important than the width of the groove is that the wood on either side of it is equal in width; this ensures that the groove is centered and that only one setup is needed to form the tenons.

One way to make this groove is to raise the saw blade ⅜ inch above the table and set the distance from the blade to the fence at ¼ inch. Using this method, however, not all the

FRAME WITH HAUNCHED MORTISE-AND-TENON JOINTS: CUTTING THE GROOVE

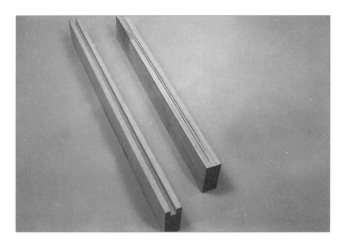

7–9. Look over the stock. Put a mark on the edge that is to be grooved.

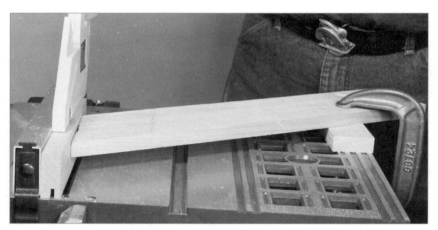

7–10. The distance from the outer edge of the work to the near side of the saw kerf is ¼ inch. The cut is made away from the fence because the throat plate opening is too large to do it the opposite way.

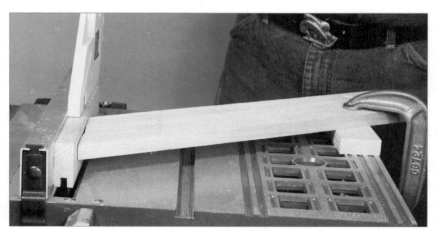

7–11. When the piece is reversed and a second cut is made, the groove is perfectly centered with ¼ inch of wood on either side. Make sure that the table always supports the workpiece.

parts can be cut with their exposed faces against the fence. Another way is to set the ¼-inch distance on the other side of the blade (7–10). Make sure that the opposite wood is supported on the throat plate for the entire cut (7–11).

Once one side of the groove has been cut, all the parts are cut again with their faces against the fence. The two sides of the groove are now equal (¼ inch wide). If stock remains between the saw kerfs, the fence can be moved slightly and another cut made.

Once the groove is cut, the stiles can be set aside. The rails now require some work, to complete the tenons. Set up the dado head as described in Setting Up a Dado Head on pages 50 and 51. Adjust the dado head to cut a ⅝-to ¾-inch-wide dado. When a rail is set on the table facedown, the dado height should equal the bottom of the groove (about ¼ inch).

The best way to find this setting is to slowly raise the dado head (7–12). Make a cut for each adjustment. Control the stock with the miter gauge. When there is a thin sliver of wood remaining between the groove and dado head, you are close to the desired setting (7–13). Cut into both faces about ⅜ inch from the end and test the fit of the tenon with the groove cut in another piece (7–14). It should fit without force. Test one or two pieces to be sure of the setting.

If satisfied with the setting, lock the height adjustment. Set the fence so that the distance from the fence to the edge of the dado head farther from the fence is one and one-half inches. Lock this setting.

Butt the end of the stock to the fence and the edge to the miter gauge. A stop can also be used for this setting. Turn on the saw. Guide the stock into the dado head and make a cut

FRAME WITH HAUNCHED MORTISE-AND-TENON JOINTS: RAIL TENONS

7–12. Slowly raise the dado head and make trial cuts on both sides of the piece. This setting is about right.

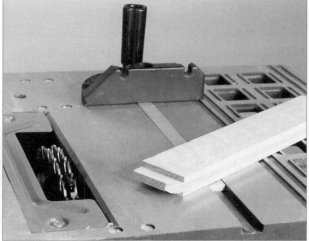

7–13. This little "feather" of wood where the tongue meets the groove indicates that the dado head must be raised only slightly.

(continued on following page)

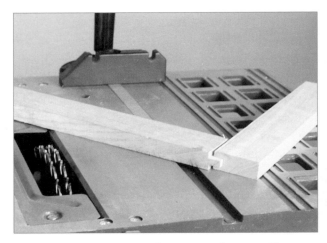

7–14. The true test is the fit between the parts. They should not have to be forced together.

7–15. Butt the stock to the fence and make the first cut. A stop can also be used on the fence if so desired.

7–16. Move away from the fence until the whole face has been cut. This will take three or four cuts.

7–17. Turn the piece over and repeat the process. Both ends of the rails must be cut.

7–18. Once both ends of all the parts have been cut, the haunch setup can be made.

(7–15). Retract the miter gauge and move the work away from the fence about the width of the dado head. Continue this process of cutting on both faces of both ends of the rails (7–16). When these cuts have been completed, a tenon will have been formed on each end of the rails (7–17 and 7–18).

Now move the fence ⅜ inch closer to the dado head and lock it in position. Raise the dado head another ¼ inch so that it will cut a dado ½ inch deep. Position the rail with its outside edge on the table, its face against the miter gauge, and its end against the fence. Turn on the saw and make the cut (7–19). Move the rail away from the fence about the width of the dado and make another cut (7–20). Continue this process until the haunch is cut (7–21).

Check the fit of the haunch with the groove (7–22). Make any needed adjustment by mov-

FRAME WITH HAUNCHED MORTISE-AND-TENON JOINTS: RAIL TENONS (CONTINUED)

7–19. Make the first cut to the rail with its edge on the table and its end butted to the fence.

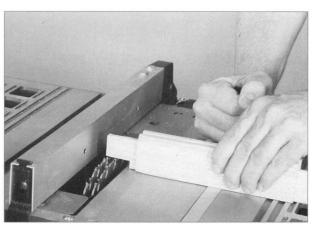

7–20. Make additional cuts while moving the end away from the fence.

7–21. Cut a haunch on both ends of the workpiece. The grooved side should be up for both cuts.

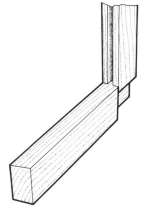

7–22. The haunch should bottom out in the groove, with no gaps where the two parts meet. Make any needed adjustments.

ing the fence. Use the rails to mark the position of the mortise on the rails. Mark the two ends of the mortise on the stiles.

The mortise can be cut in a number of ways: a series of holes with a drill bit; a mortiser; a router and a spiral upcut bit; or a doweling jig and drill bit. The depth of the mortise is 1½ inches from the edge of the stile. It may have to be cleaned out with a sharp chisel to get a good fit. If the ends of the mortise are round, the tenons can be rounded with a chisel or a file.

Dry-fit all the parts and mark them so they can be reassembled later.

Sawing a Raised Panel

If a raised panel will be added to either type of door (7–23), first the panel is prepared, and then the edges are raised.

To determine the panel size, assemble the door frame and measure the height and width of the opening. Add ½ inch to each dimension; this will be the length and width of the panel stock. With ⅜-inch grooves or rabbets, this will allow ⅛-inch movement at all edges.

It may be necessary to glue stock to size to make up the panel. Another option is to resaw thicker stock to make panel stock. Refer to Resawing on pages 110 to 112 for information on resawing stock. Stock ½ inch thick makes ideal panel stock, but ¾-inch-thick stock may also be used. Rip and crosscut panel stock to size.

Once all stock is cut to size, it should be sanded smooth on both faces. Inspect the stock and determine which face should be raised. Mark this face.

Adjust the blade ³⁄₃₂ inch above the table and lock the setting. Set the distance from the near side of the blade to the fence at 1½ inches and lock the setting (7–24). Make four kerfs in the exposed or raised face of the panel (7–25). Butt the end edges of the panel against the fence to make these cuts. Control the cross-grain cuts with the miter gauge, and control the rip cuts using a push stick.

Inspect the corners where the saw kerfs intersect. Make sure that they are the same depth. If they are not, the piece may be warped. Bear down on that portion of the panel and repeat the cut. Inspect all corners to be sure they are

***7–23.** Raised panel.*

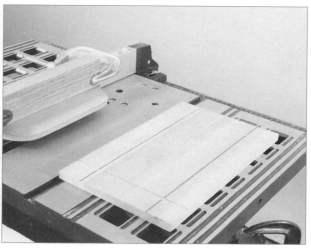

7–24. Set the distance from the fence to the near side of the fence at 1½ inches. The blade should be 3/32 inch above the table.

7–25. Make the kerf cuts in the raised face of the panel by butting the panel's end edges against the fence. Each panel requires four cuts.

the correct depth before breaking down the setup.

If the blade on the saw tilts to the right, put the fence on the left side of the blade. If the blade tilts to the left, put the fence on the right side. Attach a piece of ¾-inch sheet stock to the blade side of the fence. The piece should be eight inches wide and as long as the fence. Use screws to secure the wooden fence.

Mark the panel for the inclined cut (7–26). If you are working with ½-inch stock, the incline will start at the kerf and slant toward the back. The distance from the incline to the back of the panel at the edge (remaining thickness) will be equal to the width of the groove (about ¼ inch). This line represents an incline of about six degrees.

If you are working with ¾-inch stock, the angle

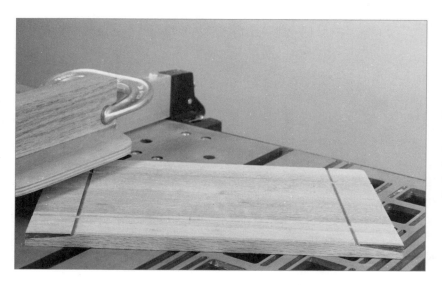

7–26. Lay out the incline on the edge of the panel. There should be a ¼-inch edge left after the incline is sawn. The line extends to the bottom of the saw kerf.

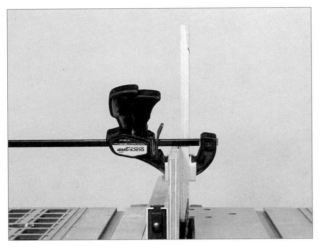

7–27. Clamp the work to the auxiliary fence for layout purposes. Position the fence so that the layout line on the work is lined up with the blade.

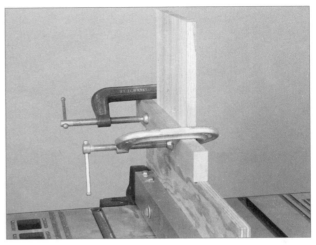

7–28. This straightedge is clamped to the panel. It acts as a vertical miter gauge and takes any warp out of the panel.

will also be about six degrees. The line will start at the bottom of the kerf and slant back to the ¼-inch mark. This mark is measured from the face. Once the incline is cut on the ¾-inch stock, the edge will be about ½ inch thick. The edge on the ½-inch stock will be about ¼ inch thick.

Position the panel on the saw (7–27). The edge of the panel should be on the table and the back should be touching the wooden auxil-

iary fence. Move the fence until the blade is positioned correctly to make the cut. The blade should touch the bottom of the saw kerf that is cut into the face of the panel. If you are uncertain of where the layout line is, make the panel oversized and slowly cut it to size.

Once the position is set and the fence is locked, a ¾-inch straightedge slightly longer than the panel is positioned on top of the auxiliary fence (7–28). The panel is then clamped

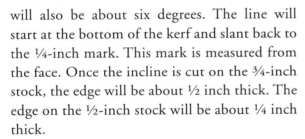

7–29. The feather-board goes above the blade and helps push the stock against the fence. It also acts as a barrier between the operator and the blade.

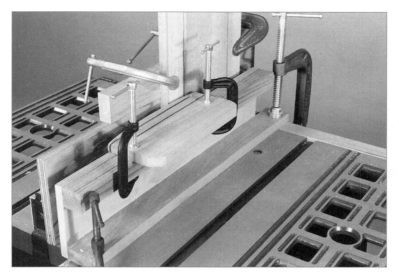

7–30. *In this setup, a barrier is clamped to the table and a slightly different type of featherboard is being used. This featherboard holds the stock against the fence and makes operator contact with the blade almost impossible.*

to the fence with C-clamps. The clamping action will bring the panel into a true plane. It will also act as a control device and prevent the cut panel from falling into the opening in the throat plate.

The final setup is the featherboard (7–29 and 7–30). The featherboard is positioned on a spacer block and butted against the panel over

the saw blade. It is held in place with two C-clamps. The spacer elevates the featherboard to a height above the saw blade. The featherboard thus acts as a barrier between the operator and the blade. It also holds the panel firmly against the auxiliary fence.

Position the panel against the fence and clear of the blade (7–31 and 7–32). The straightedge

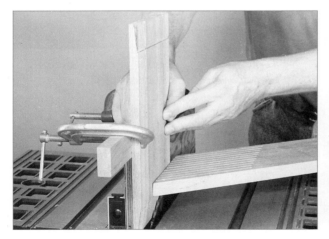

7–31. *The panel is held against the fence while the cut is made. This is a rip cut and it may require a coarser blade (less than 40 teeth) to eliminate burning.*

7–32. *This setup makes raised-panel-cutting safe and efficient. Push the stock completely past the blade, and then lift it off the fence. Shut off the saw. When the blade stops, move the clamps and straightedge to the opposite edge.*

7–33. The edge barely fits in the groove. After sanding, it should be a perfect fit.

should rest on top of the fence. Turn on the saw and guide the workpiece into the blade. Once the cut is complete and the panel clears the blade, lift it up and clear off the blade. Turn off the saw and allow the blade to come to a complete stop.

Move the panel to another edge or end, and reset the straightedge. Fasten the clamps securely. After the second setup, you will be clamping to an inclined surface. Some of the pieces that have been cut off can then be used as clamp pads. Repeat the cutting process as outlined for all four edges. The edge of the panel should now barely fit into the groove in the edge of the door frame (7–33). Once the inclined edges are sanded, the panel will fit farther into the frame. This is discussed in the following section.

Sanding the Panel

Now that all frames have been fitted, it is time to sand them. (Refer to Chapter 8 for information on sanding.) Then they will be fitted with the mating panels. At this point, the panels are oversized for the groove in the edge of the frame (7–34) and they may have burn marks,

7–34. The panels are oversized and may have burn marks that will need to be sanded away.

so sanding will need to be done. If the frame has lap joints, the panel should drop into the rabbet with ⅛ inch of clearance on each end and edge, so this area of the frame will not have to be sanded.

The inclined surfaces have not been sanded yet, no matter which type of frame has been made. Now is the time to do this (7–35). The raised area is bordered by a straight square shoulder. This is left over from the saw kerf cut into the face of the panel. It is important that

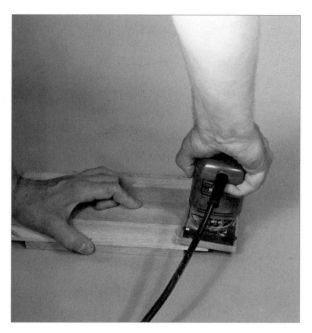

7–35. An orbital sander that uses a one-quarter- to one-sixth sheet of sandpaper works well for sanding the inclined surface. Set the panel on a block to raise it off the work surface. The sander can now do its job.

this square shoulder *not* be sanded. This shoulder defines the raised area. Any sanding along the shoulder will detract from the door's appearance.

An orbital sander, which uses a one-quarter to one-sixth sheet of sandpaper, is the best choice for the task. Choose 60- to 80-grit garnet abrasive for the initial sanding. If the scratches from the saw blade are small and fine, 80-grit sandpaper can be used to start the job. Coarser scratches will require 60-grit sandpaper. Clamp the panel to a workbench or other surface. Sand the edges with an orbital sander. The edge of the sander can ride along the shoulder of the raised area. This will serve as a guide.

Sand all four surfaces carefully. Observe the intersection of the two inclined surfaces at the

corner. A miter line should be formed between the inside raised shoulder and the outside corner. The sanding action can encourage these surfaces to meet correctly.

After all sanding has been done with the coarser paper, repeat the process with a 20 grit-or finer abrasive, for example, 60- to 80-grit, 80- to 100-grit, 100- to 120-grit. Sanding should cease at about 120-grit on long grain and 150-grit on end grain. Hand-sand these surfaces after machine-sanding them. Finer sanding is done to the end grain to ensure that the stain used on the door will be uniform in color on all surfaces.

Block-sand the raised area of the panel with 120-grit abrasive (7–36). Keep half of the block on the surface at all times. This will prevent the shoulder from rounding. Avoid over-sanding the face of the panel. Most sanding should have been done before the face of the panel was kerfed.

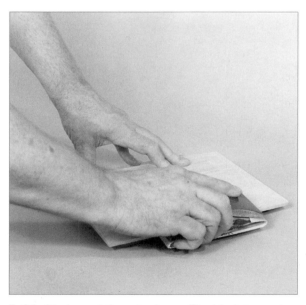

7–36. Block-sand the raised area. The block prevents the crisp square corners from being rounded.

Fitting the Parts

The panels should now be fitted into the appropriate frame. The sanding should have reduced the thickness of the edge so that it fits into the frame nicely. If the panel is too large for the groove, it can be adjusted easily.

The easiest way to adjust the fit is to shave a small amount off the back of the panel along the edge with a block plane or orbital sander. If there is too much material for this approach, the back of the panel can be rabbeted. Refer to Rabbet Joints on pages 57 and 58 for information on cutting a rabbet using a dado head. Set the fence to expose ⅜ inch of the panel. Take light cuts until the panel simply slides into the groove.

Fit all the parts together without glue to be sure they fit properly. If there is glue on any of the parts and they do not fit together, adjusting the fit becomes complicated. The glue could set up before the parts are positioned correctly. This could result in a large amount of rework.

With either lap-joint frames or mortise-and-tenon-joint frames, it is best to stain the panel before assembling the door. This ensures that there will be no unstained edges showing if the panel shrinks.

Sand all the inside edges of the frames (7–37). Pay particular attention to the edges of the grooves. They can be rounded slightly to better take the stain. If there is a rabbet joint on the backside of a lap-joint frame door, sand, stain, and finish it properly. If there is a glass or mirror in the rabbet, it will be visible through the glass or as a reflection in the mirror. Treat these rabbets as exposed edges.

When gluing up mortise-and-tenon doors, keep the glue off the panels. The panel must be free to move in the frame. If it becomes glued into position, it could split if the panel shrinks and cannot move. For best results, brush the glue on the mortise and tenon, keeping it away from the inside corner where it could squeeze out.

Clamp the door in position and check for squareness (7–38). Make any adjustments quickly, before the glue sets up. For best results, allow any glue that squeezes out to harden before removal. Wiping glue away with a damp towel only serves to move it around and make a bigger mess.

After the glue cures, the clamp can be removed and the glue can be cleaned off. The panel should be centered in the opening. Once it is centered, it is held in place with two ⅝-inch brads.

From the back of the door, drive a brad through the groove and raised panel. The

7–37. Sand the inside edges of the frames. Pay attention to the grooves. Slightly rounding them will make it easier for the stain to penetrate.

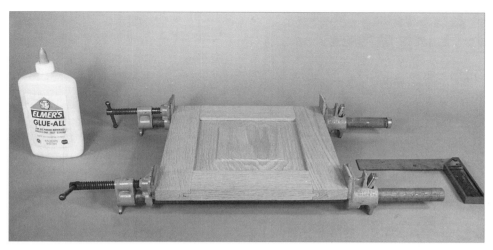

7–38. *Clamp the door and check for squareness. Do not let the glue get on the panel. The panel should not be glued in the frame; it should be able to move. Refer to page 134 for general gluing instructions.*

brad is driven on the centerline at the top and bottom of the panel. For hardwoods, it will be necessary to drill a pilot hole for the nail. Be careful not to drill through the front of the door.

If a rabbet is required around the outside edge of the door, it can be cut now (7–39). Refer to Rabbet Joints on pages 57 and 58 for information on making the rabbet with a dado head. The rabbet must be ⅜ inch x ⅜ inch.

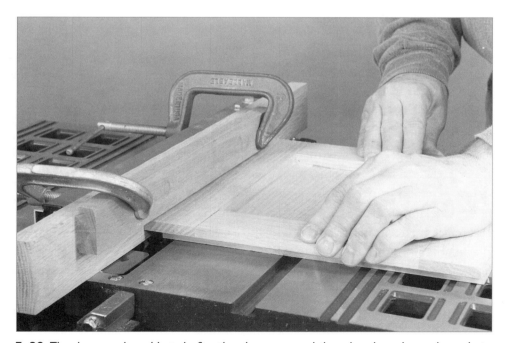

7–39. *The door can be rabbeted after the glue cures and the edges have been cleaned up.*

A Word About Woodworking Glues

There are many types of common woodworking glues available. Following is a discussion of some of the best ones to use for woodworking projects.

Polyvinyl resin glue (often referred to as "white glue") is a strong general-purpose glue that dries clean and is useful for the assembly of nonstressed joints. It does not require mixing, has an assembly time (the time a woodworker has to clamp the pieces before the glue hardens, or cures) of about six minutes and requires 1½ hours of clamping time (the time the glued pieces must be held together under pressure). It is water-soluble and should not be used in damp or wet conditions. The glue will also soften when heated.

Aliphatic resin glue, which is light yellow, is very similar to polyvinyl resin. The differences are that it is stronger and that less creep takes place when it is used. (Creep is the sliding of pieces that can occur during clamping.) Aliphatic resin glue has an assembly time of about six minutes and requires 30 minutes to one hour of clamping time.

Plastic resin glue is sold in powder form and requires mixing. Its pot life– the length of time it can be used after mixing– is approximately four hours. It is water- and heat-resistant, has a 10- to 15-minute assembly time, and requires one to two hours of clamping time.

Hide glue, which is made from animal hides and bones, is available in both flake and liquid forms. The liquid glue is more popular because the flakes take time and require heat to mix. Liquid hide glue is good for use on interior furniture and when repairing or assembling veneer.

Hide glue, which leaves a light-brown glue line, is water-soluble and should not be used in damp and wet conditions. Its assembly time is 10 to 15 minutes, and it requires a clamping time of at least three hours.

Urea Resin glue is good for interior and exterior woodworking projects. It comes in a plastic form and must be mixed. It has a four-hour pot life, a 10-to-15 minute assembly time, and a clamping time of one to three hours.

PREPARING JOINERY FOR GLUING

To ensure that the glue works well, follow these instructions:

❶ Make sure the mating surfaces have no gaps.

❷ Plane but do not sand all glue surfaces. Sanding can seal the wood and make adhesion difficult.

❸ When gluing a mortise-and-tenon or dowel joint together, check the "dry fit" first. The pieces should be snug, but not too tight. If the dry fit is tight without glue, it may be impossible to assemble the pieces after gluing. This is because the water in the glue will cause the wood to swell.

❹ When assembling several pieces, try to divide the job into several smaller units. Large assemblies are difficult with fast-curing glues. If a large assembly must be glued in one operation, choose a glue with a long assembly time.

❺ When end-grain gluing two pieces, double-coat both pieces before gluing. This allows the glue to penetrate into the end grain. Reinforce end-grain joinery whenever possible.

8 Sanding Techniques

Disc sanders and table saws both have a table with a miter gauge to control stock. Therefore, if the blade on a table saw is replaced with a sanding disc, all the sanding operations accomplished with a disc sander can be done with a table saw without the need to add another piece of equipment to the shop. These operations can include disc-sanding outside curves and straight edges when the sanding disc is mounted on the arbor, and sanding chamfers and bevels when the disc is tilted.

There are accessory discs available for most table saws (8–1). They are made from tempered steel or cast aluminum and vary in size from about six to ten inches in diameter. A 10-inch table saw would use a sanding disc with a maximum diameter of 10 inches.

Sanding can be done either freehand or with the use of a miter gauge or fence. Each technique is described below in Sanding Guidelines.

SANDING GUIDELINES

❶ Read Safety Techniques, which follows, before sanding.

❷ Install the sanding disc in the same manner as a blade. (Refer to Changing Blades on pages 42 to 45.) Use the correct saw blade throat plate.

❸ If you are freehand sanding—that is, you are using only your hands to control the workpiece (8–2)—sand with the portion of the disc that is going toward the table. This will push the workpiece down on the table while sanding is taking place. Keep the work moving, and use all of the disc. This will spread the abrasive wear and reduce burning or abrasive-loading.

8–1. Sanding discs can be mounted on a table saw in the same way as a blade. Refer to Changing Blades on pages 42 to 45.

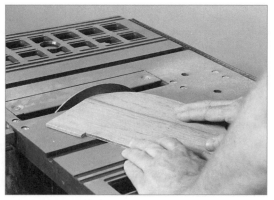

8–2. When freehand-sanding, sand on the portion of the disc that is going downhill. To reduce burning or abrasive-loading, keep the work moving.

(continued on following page)

SANDING GUIDELINES (CONTINUED)

❹ Either the miter gauge or the fence can be used to control stock during sanding. The miter gauge controls the stock and ensures that the correct angle setting is being used. As with freehand sanding, be sure to keep the stock moving while sanding (8–3). This will reduce burning and abrasive-loading.

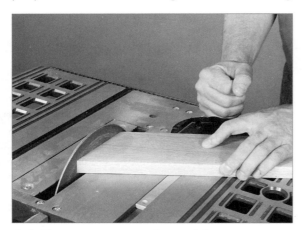

8–3. The miter gauge can be used for precision-sanding at any angle. To prevent burning and abrasive-loading, keep the work moving.

❺ If parallel edges are being sanded, the fence can be used to guide the stock. Do not trap the work between the disc and fence. The abrasives on the disc should just brush the workpiece. The safest setup incorporates the guard for this operation (8–4). This reduces the chance of kickback and contact with the disc. Position yourself away from the kickback zone while edge-sanding with the fence as a guide.

8–4. When edge-sanding, do not pinch the workpiece. The abrasive should only lightly brush the edge of the workpiece. The guard will help control any kickback and make contact with the blade unlikely.

❻ The most common mistake made when disc-sanding is to use too fine an abrasive. Because of the high rpms of the disc, fine abrasives cannot clear the wood chips quickly enough. This causes heat and will ultimately burn the abrasive. It is important that the right type of abrasive be used for the job. Refer to Determining Abrasive Grit on page 137 for this information.

Safety Techniques

In most cases, the accessory disc will have abrasives on both sides—one coarse, and the other fine. Therefore, before sanding, consider a means of dust collection. The fine dust generated by the abrasives can create a mess. It can also be harmful to humans, so be sure to wear a dust mask. Refer to Dust-Collection System on pages 23 to 26.

While a sanding disc may not seem as dangerous as a blade, there are some hazards. Hands should not make contact with the disc. It will remove skin quickly. Fingers could also become wedged between the rotating disc and throat plate. This could cause serious injury. There should be a four- to six-inch margin between the operator and the abrasive disc at all times; this should allow for plenty of reaction time.

DETERMINING ABRASIVE GRIT

Type of Work	Abrasive
General-Duty Sanding	60 to 80 grit
Sanding on Rougher Work	40 grit
Sanding on Finer Work	100 or 120 grit

Replacing Abrasives

When the abrasives on a sanding disc wear out, they can be replaced easily. The old disc is peeled away from the metal backing. If contact cement has been used on the old sheet, it will peel off easily. If other types of glue were used, the abrasive sheet will not peel off easily and some residue may remain (8–5). If this occurs,

8–5. Notice the residue left on this disc from the glue. It can be removed with the sharpened piece of stock behind the disc.

clean the metal disc with mineral spirits or other solvents or by using the method shown in 8–6. This consists of mounting the sanding disc on the table saw using the correct throat plate; turning the saw on with the disc at full height; and using a sharpened piece of hardwood to scrape the disc, pressing the wood lightly against the disc. Continue this process until the disc is clean.

8–6. Press the piece of stock against the turning disc. Work from the outside toward the center.

Whichever technique is used, make sure that the disc is completely clean before replacing the abrasive with a peel-and-stick type of abrasive (8–7 to 8–10). These abrasives are the easiest to work with.

REPLACING SANDING-DISC ABRASIVES

8–7. All the glue residue should be removed before new abrasives are applied.

(continued on following page)

REPLACING SANDING-DISC ABRASIVES (CONTINUED)

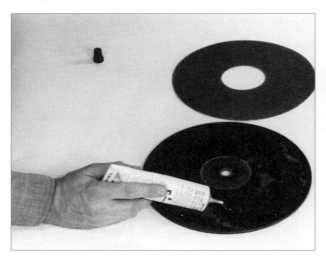

8–8. The contact cement should be applied liberally to the surface of the disc.

8–9. The disc is pressed into the contact cement and lifted up. This allows the solvents to evaporate.

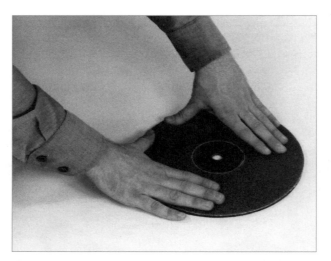

8–10. After 30 seconds, lay the abrasive down on the disc and smooth out any bubbles.

9 Molding Techniques

The molding head is an attachment for the table saw that allows the operator to make decorative profiles on the face, edge, or end of a piece of wood. The various molding heads are designed to use one to three cutters (9–1). The best molding heads use three. They will produce the smoothest results and are less likely to kick back. Each of the cutters in a molding head has the same decorative profile and is held to the head by threaded fasteners.

Some table saws cannot accommodate a molding head. If the arbor is not long enough to secure the molding head, the head cannot be used. For safe operation of the molding head, all of the threads of the arbor nut must be engaged with the arbor. Refer to Safety Guidelines on page 146 before making any molding cuts.

9–1. *The Sears Craftsman molding head on the left uses two cutters. The one on the right uses three. The two-cutter head is usually used on smaller, low-powered table saws.*

Inserting Molding-Head Cutters

Follow these procedures to insert molding-head cutters:

1. Select the cutters that will be used and insert them into the head (9–2). Make sure that they are inserted properly. They should all be point-ing the same way. Most molding heads are designed so that the cutters can be inserted only one way. Usually there is some indication on the cutters as to the way that they should be mounted.

2. Look over the cutters during insertion. They should not be used if they are nicked or damaged in any way. Tighten the fasteners securely (9–3).

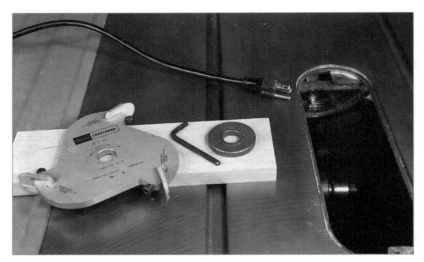

9–2. Look over the cutters while inserting them into the head. They should be free of nicks and should all face the same way. Make sure they have the same profile. Notice the fastener on the cutter head (with the attached cutters), the Allen wrench used to tighten the fastener, and the arbor nut.

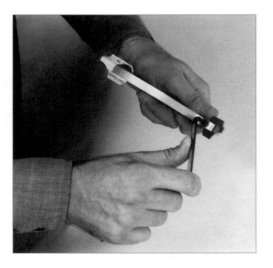

9–3. Make sure that the fasteners holding the cutters are locked securely. Check them periodically to make sure that they are tight.

3. Disconnect the power to the saw and remove the blade. Mount the molding head on the saw. In some cases, a spacer goes on the arbor first. Be sure to check the instructions that came with the molding head. Make sure that the head is mounted so that the flat face of the cutter touches the wood first. Tighten the arbor nut securely; it may not be possible to use the arbor washer due to the width of the molding head. Make sure that the entire arbor nut is engaged with the threads of the arbor. Do not operate the molding head if the arbor nut is not totally engaged (9–4).

4. Install the molding head throat plate. It will have an opening that will accommodate the cutters. Turn the molding head over by hand to be sure that it clears the throat plate (9–5). Do not operate the molding head without the appropriate throat plate.

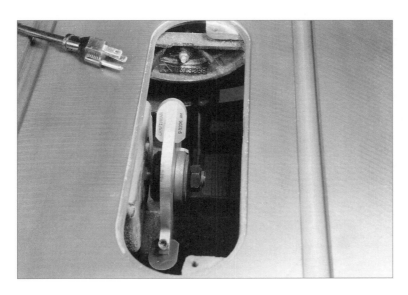

9–4. All of the arbor nut must be engaged with the threads on the arbor. Do not operate the molding head if the arbor nut is not fully engaged.

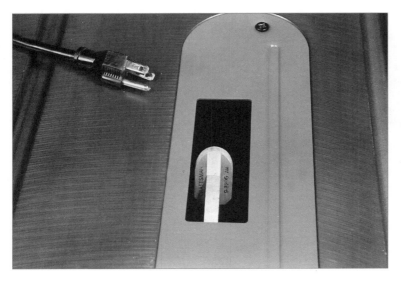

9–5. Check to be sure that the molding head clears the throat plate. If the height of the molding head is changed, make this check again.

A wooden throat plate can also be made to accommodate any molding operation. To make one, use any throat plate that fits the saw as a model (9–6 and 9–7). Use stock that is as thick as the throat plate or slightly thinner. Rip the stock to the width of the throat plate. Lay out the curved ends with the throat plate. Cut the curved ends with a band saw or saber saw. Disc-sand the curves to the layout line.

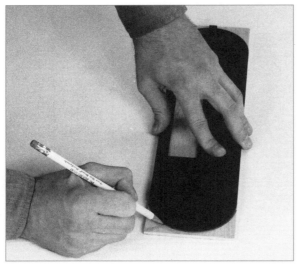

9–6. *When making an auxiliary throat plate, use the metal throat plate as a template. Rip the stock to throat-plate width before laying out the ends.*

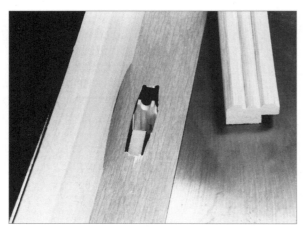

9–7. *The wooden throat plate shown here is better suited to molding work than the standard throat plate.*

Holes may have to be drilled and tapped to hold the throat plate in place. Locate these holes in the lugs that support the throat plate. Drill the plate to match these holes. Anchor the throat plate with flat-head machine screws. If the plate is too low, use tape, paper, or veneer to raise it.

The hole in the throat plate is cut with the molding head. Mount the molding head and drop it beneath the table. Install the throat plate, turn on the saw, and slowly raise the moving cutter into the throat plate. The hole made in the plate will match the blade or cutter perfectly. If the arbor is to be tilted, the molding head must be lowered beneath the table, tilted, and then raised into the throat plate while it is moving.

Never attempt to hold a throat plate in place while cutting into it. The throat plate must be secured in place.

Face Molding

Cutting a profile into the face of a board with a molding head is much like making a rip cut. A fence is used to control the workpiece. Do the following to cut face molding:

1. Make sure that the workpiece is at least 12 inches long, wide enough to be supported by the table throughout the cut, and at least ¾ inch thick. Use featherboards to control the workpiece; they should be clamped to the table or fence. Two or more featherboards can be used.

2. Position the fence for the cut that will be made (9–8).

3. Lower the molding head so that a light cut will be made. Harder woods will require an even lighter cut than soft woods.

4. Turn on the saw and guide the wood into the cutter. Stand clear of the kickback zone during the cut. Use a push stick to complete the cut (9–9).

5. Push the work completely past the cutters and turn off the saw. If resistance is being experienced while you are cutting, either too

heavy of a cut is being made or the cutters are dull.

6. Take lighter cuts while progressing to the layout line (9–10). The lightest cut should be when the layout line is approached. This will improve the quality of the cut (9–11).

CUTTING FACE MOLDING

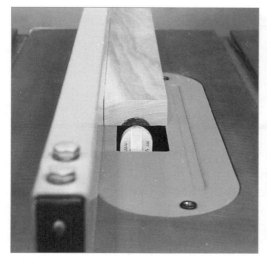

9–8. Position the fence to put the profile in the right spot. Lock the fence once it is positioned.

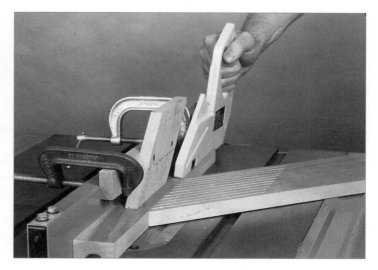

9–9. Use a push stick to make the cut. Push the work past the cutter head and shut off the saw.

9–10. Take lighter cuts while progressing toward the layout line. This will improve the quality of the final profile.

(continued on following page)

CUTTING FACE MOLDING (CONTINUED)

9–11. *A smooth profile is achieved by taking light cuts and feeding the workpiece at a moderate speed.*

EDGE MOLDING

An edge molding setup requires an auxiliary fence. The wooden auxiliary fence should be ¾ inch thick or greater. It should be at least as wide and long as the metal fence. Any portion of the cutter that will not be used for cutting edge molding is actually in the wooden fence.

Follow these procedures when cutting edge molding:

1. Using wood screws, attach the wooden fence to the metal fence (9–12). There are usually holes in the metal fence for this purpose. Position the wooden portion of the fence over any part of the cutters that will not be used and lock the metal fence to the table. Make sure that no part of the cutters will contact the metal fence.

2. Make sure that the orbit of the cutters is low enough to clear the wood before you turn on the saw. Then turn on the saw and slowly raise the molding head into the wooden fence. Raise the molding head slightly above the desired height and then lower it to the desired height (9–13). This will prevent the cutters from rubbing on the fence during all of the cuts and will keep the cutters sharper longer.

3. Adjust the fence and cutter to the edge profile that will be cut (9–14). Add featherboards and a barrier to make the operation safer (9–15). Lower the molding head and make the first cut. This cut is also made in the same manner as a rip cut. Use a push stick to guide the workpiece (9–16).

4. Guide the workpiece completely past the cutter head and turn off the saw. Raise the cutter and make additional cuts until the profile is complete.

End-Grain Molding

When molding is being cut on the ends of the workpiece, the same setup procedures described

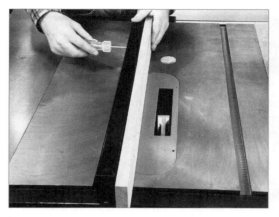

9–12. A wooden auxiliary fence is being attached to the metal fence. Use a straight-grained hardwood for this purpose. Part of the fence will be cut away by the molding cutter shown here.

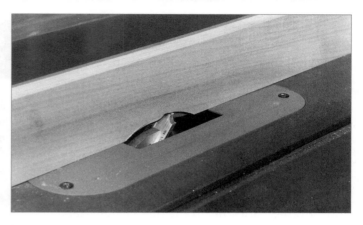

9–13. Raise the cutter above the layout line, and then lower it slightly. This will prevent the cutter from overheating or dulling prematurely.

9–14. Position the fence and cutter head. Lock the fence and lower the cutter head before making a cut.

9–15. The featherboards and barrier make this cutting operation safer.

9–16. Use a push stick to complete the cut. Push the work completely past the cutter head, and turn off the saw.

above are used, except that no featherboards or push stick are used. A miter gauge is used to guide the wood into the molding head.

Do the following when shaping the ends of boards:

1. Set the head for a light cut. Butt the end of the workpiece to the fence and the edge against the head of the miter gauge (9–17).

2. Turn on the saw and guide the miter gauge and workpiece forward. If the piece is "chattering," take a lighter cut. Continue the process until the profile is complete.

3. Start on the ends of the workpiece when all four edges of a workpiece are being cut. This way, any tear-out on the end can be removed when the edges are shaped.

4. Do all shaping with the end or edge of the workpiece touching the fence. The workpiece should never be trapped between the fence and cutter. This exposes more cutter and can contribute to a kickback.

SAFETY GUIDELINES

Experience has shown that two types of accidents are generally associated with molding heads: kickback and/or contact with the cutters. Do the following to prevent these accidents from occurring:

❶ Make barrier guards whenever possible, and use featherboards and push sticks to help control the workpiece.

❷ Take light cuts. Too heavy a cut can result in a kickback or can cause the feeding hand to make contact with the cutter.

❸ Do not use a throat plate with an opening larger than the workpiece. The workpiece could fall into the opening, resulting in kickback or cutter breakage.

❹ Do not work on short or narrow stock. These put hands too close to the cutter head and could cause stock to shatter or kick back.

❺ Do not trap the workpiece between the fence and cutter head. This too can cause a kickback and expose the entire cutter head, even when only a portion of the cutter head is being used.

❻ Avoid contact between the cutter head and metal fence. This can cause cutter breakage and possible injury from flying metal pieces.

9–17. The miter gauge and fence control the shaping of end grain. Take a light cut and use a barrier.

Reading the information contained in the section Factors That Contribute to Woodworking Accidents will give the table-saw user an understanding of the general conditions that lead to accidents with power tools. Following the instructions in Table-Saw Safety Techniques will enable him or her to avoid accidents with the table saw.

Factors That Contribute to Woodworking Accidents

One or more of the following factors will most likely play a part in accidents that occur when woodworking:

1. *Working while tired or taking medication.* Accidents are most likely to happen when the woodworker is tired, so stop and take a break whenever this occurs. Use of medication and alcohol can affect perception and reception time.

2. *Rushing the job.* Trying to finish a job in a hurry leads to errors and accidents. The stress of rushing the job also leads to early fatigue.

3. *Inattention to the job.* Daydreaming or thinking about another job while you are operating power tools can lead to accidents. Repetitive cuts lend themselves to daydreaming, so be doubly careful when making them.

4. *Distractions.* Conversing with others, unfamiliar noises, and doors opening or closing are all distractions in the shop. Shut off the power equipment before engaging in conversation or investigating an unfamiliar noise. Also, never surprise someone who is working with any power tool.

5. *A dirty or cluttered work area.* This will provide tripping hazards and excess dust that can be a breathing hazard. Keep the shop neat and clean. It is more pleasant and safer to work in a clean area.

TABLE-SAW SAFETY TECHNIQUES Specific safety techniques should be followed when using a table saw, in order to ensure its safe operation:
❶ Set the saw at a comfortable height. Most operators prefer a height of 34 to 36 inches.
❷ Make sure that the saw does not rock and that it has been leveled properly. Whenever possible, anchor the saw to the floor.
❸ Make sure that a grounded outlet of the correct amperage is close by. This outlet should be below the saw so that the cord does not interfere with the stock being cut.

(continued on following page)

TABLE-SAW SAFETY TECHNIQUES (*CONTINUED*)

❹ Make sure that the workshop has adequate lighting. Adequate lighting makes it much safer to operate a table saw. Shadows and dim lighting increase operator fatigue and measurement errors.

❺ Make sure that the area surrounding the table saw is ample enough to accommodate large pieces of stock. Traffic should be routed away from the kickback zone, which is in line with the blade on the infeed side near where the operator stands. In the event of a kickback, this is where the stock is most likely to go.

❻ Keep the floor around the saw free of cut-offs and debris. These can cause someone to trip or slip.

❼ Wear the proper safety equipment and clothing. Always wear protective glasses when operating the table saw (10–1). If the area is noisy, wear earplugs or muffs to preserve hearing and minimize fatigue. When using a fine-toothed blade, wear a dust mask to protect your lungs. Better yet, install a dust collector. Refer to Dust-Collection System on pages 23 to 26.

10–1. Protective equipment such as goggles and earmuffs should be worn when the table saw is being used.

Gloves can be used to handle rough lumber, but never wear them (or other loose clothing) when operating the table saw. Your hand could easily be pulled into the blade if the blade caught the glove (or other loose clothing). Rings and watches should be removed, for the same reasons.

❽ Whenever possible, use the guard. The guard minimizes the chance of kickbacks with the splitter and anti-kickback pawls. It also makes contact with the saw blade very difficult (10–2). In addition, use two push sticks — one in each hand. Working with two push sticks ensures that you will not grab anything because your hands are full already. This eliminates the temptation to reach over the blade.

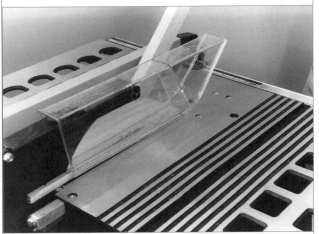

10–2. The guard should be used for all possible operations. The operator should position himself away from the kickback zone (immediately behind the blade). The push stick helps keep hands away from the blade. Note the blade height: It is less than ¹/4 inch above the workpiece.

❾ Keep the blade low. Set the blade height so that it is no more than ¼ inch higher than stock thickness. This minimizes the amount of exposed blade. Less blade in the stock also reduces the possibility of kickback caused by pinching.

❿ Keep the blade sharp. A sharp blade makes the table saw much safer to use. A dull or an incorrect blade increases the chance of kickback. It also requires more cutting force. This excess force can throw the operator off balance and lead to an accident.

TABLE-SAW SAFETY TECHNIQUES *(CONTINUED)*

⓫ Inspect the stock. Before sawing any stock, look it over. Loose knots, twist, cupping, and rough or wet lumber can mean trouble. Loose knots can be ejected by the saw blade. Rough, warped, or wet lumber can cause kickbacks.

Small pieces can also cause problems. Cutting them puts hands too close to the blade. Use push sticks and other devices to support small pieces. If possible, cut the small pieces that are needed from a larger piece.

⓬ Position yourself properly. Stand to the side of the blade to avoid kickbacks. Make sure you have firm footing and balance when operating the table saw. Avoid overreaching and reaching over the blade.

⓭ Guard against accidental starting. Make any adjustments to the table saw with the power off. It is too easy to make an adjustment error that could cause an accident when the power is on. Make repairs, change blades, and install dado heads with the power disconnected. Otherwise, a serious accident could occur. Lay the power cord plug on top of the table saw to ensure it will not come on accidentally (10–3).

⓮ Use control devices. Devices such as push sticks and featherboards make handling stock safer. These devices get close to the stock and control it. Keep them near the saw at all times.

⓯ Keep your hands away from the blade. Keeping hands a safe distance (four to six inches) from the blade allows a margin for error (10–4). When hands are a safe distance from the blade, there is always time to react to hazardous situations. Never reach for scraps or cutoffs that are near the blade. Clear the table saw only after the blade has come to a complete stop.

10–4. The table-saw user should keep his or her hands four to six inches away from the blade, so that there is time to react to a hazardous situation.

⓰ Avoid cutting freehand. Control crosscuts using the table and miter gauge. Rip cuts are controlled using the table and fence. The true surface must touch the table, rip fence, or miter gauge.

⓱ Think about the job. When performing a new operation, think about the job before beginning. Ask yourself, "What could happen when I ...?" Questions of this nature help to identify and avoid accident-producing situations. If you have a premonition of trouble, stop! Avoid any job that gives you a bad feeling. Try setting up the job another way, or ask an experienced operator for his opinion.

⓲ Know your saw. Read the owner's manual and understand it before operating the saw. All saws are different; make sure you understand the one being used.

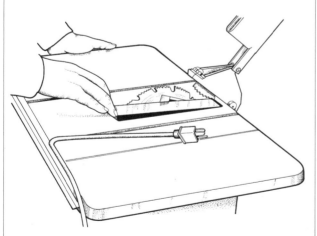

10–3. When making adjustments to the table saw, disconnect the power. Lay the power cord on top of the table saw to verify that the saw will not come on accidentally.

Glossary

Arbor The metal shaft of the table saw on which the circular-saw blade is mounted. Refer to Types of Table Saw on pages 13 to 16.

Bench Saw A saw with a blade less than 10 inches in diameter and with a small table surface. Refer to Types of Table Saw on pages 13 to 16.

Bevel An inclined surface that goes from the face of a piece of stock to another face. Refer to Edge Miters and Chamfers on pages 86 and 87.

Box Joints (also referred to as finger joints) Corner joints made up of mating fingers. The fingers slip together to form a strong joint. Refer to Box or Finger Joints on pages 62 to 66.

Cabinet Saw A saw with a blade 10 inches in diameter or greater and which has a metal cabinet as a base. Refer to Types of Table Saw on pages 13 to 16.

Carbide-Tipped Blade A blade with teeth made from small pieces of carbide. Carbide-tipped blades are much harder and more brittle than those used for conventional blades. They come in the following classifications: rip, crosscut, hollow-ground, and plywood. Refer to Tool-Steel and Carbide-Tipped Blades on pages 37 to 39.

Chamfers Inclined surfaces that go from a face to an edge of a board. Refer to Edge Miters and Chamfers on pages 86 and 87.

Coarse Blade A blade with large teeth, designed for heavy, fast, or less delicate work.

Combination Blade A blade used for ripping and crosscutting. Refer to Blade Overview Chart on page 41.

Compound Miter A miter created when the stock is angled or inclined from its true plane. Refer to Compound Miters on pages 87 to 89.

Contractor Saws Motor-driven saws with cast-iron or die-cast tables. Refer to Types of Table Saw on pages 13 to 16.

Cove Cut A curved recess cut into a piece of stock. Refer to Cove Cuts on pages 106 to 110.

Crosscut A cut made across the grain of the workpiece. Refer to Crosscuts on pages 80 to 82.

Crosscut Blade A blade designed specifically to make fast, smooth crosscuts. Refer to Blade Overview Chart on page 41.

Dado A U-shaped channel made with or across the grain of the workpiece. Refer to

Common Dadoes on pages 54 to 57 and Dadoes on pages 94 to 100.

Dado Head A blade or blades mounted in a hub and sometimes used with chippers that cut dadoes and rabbets. Refer to Dado Heads on pages 49 to 68.

Dead Man A device used to support long or wide pieces of stock being cut on the table saw.

Deflection A condition in which the circular-saw blade bounces away from or flutters in the workpiece.

Featherboards Commercial or user-made accessories that hold stock against the fence or table near the blade and keep hands out of the cutting area. Refer to Featherboards on pages 26 to 28.

Feed Speed The speed at which the stock is fed into the table-saw blade.

Fence A device used to control stock during rip cuts. Refer to Fence on page 21.

Fine Blade A blade with small teeth designed for delicate work.

Flooring Blade A specialty blade used for jobs where occasional nails may be encountered. Refer to Blade Overview Chart on page 41.

Frame-and-Panel Door A door that has two horizontal parts (rails), two vertical parts (stiles), and a panel. Refer to Door-Making Techniques on pages 117 to 134.

Guard A safety component on the table saw that protects the operator from contact with the saw. See Guard on pages 18 to 20.

Hardboard A wood material used for drawer bottoms, panel backing, and siding and cabinet parts. Refer to Sheet Stock Overview on page 72.

Hollow-Ground Blade (Planer Blade) A blade with no set. The sides of the blade are recessed for clearance in the kerf. Hollow-ground blades should be used to cut miters and compound miters, but not for heavy ripping.

Infeed Side The operator's side of the table saw.

Kerf The cut made by a circular-saw blade. It must be larger than the saw-blade thickness.

Kickback A condition in which a piece of stock is flung back at the operator at great speed. Usually, the stock becomes trapped between the rotating blade and a stationary object such as a fence or guard. Refer to Preventing Kickback on pages 72 to 74.

Miter Cut An angular cut made across the face, end, or edge of the workpiece. Most miter cuts are made at 45-degree angles, so that when the two pieces are joined they form a 90-degree angle. Refer to Miter Cuts on pages 83 to 89.

Miter Gauge A table-saw component that controls solid stock when it is crosscut, small pieces of sheet stock, and stock on which angular cuts such as miters are being made, for example, picture-frame stock. Refer to Miter Gauge on pages 20 and 21 and Specialty Miter Gauge on page 31.

Molding Decorative profiles made on the face, edge, or end of a piece of wood. Refer to Molding Techniques on pages 139 to 146.

Molding Head A cutting device to which cutters are fastened that is used to shape stock on the table saw. See Molding Techniques on pages 139 to 146.

Mortise-and-Tenon Joint A joint made up of two parts. The mortise is a slot or hole cut into one piece. The tenon is the mating piece that fits into the mortise. Refer to Tenons on pages 102 to 104, Through Mortises on pages 104 to 106, and Making a Frame with Haunched Mortise-and-Tenon Joints on pages 121 to 126.

Oriented Strand Board Sheet stock, used primarily in building construction, which is made of large pieces of wood that have been formed into sheets. Refer to Sheet Stock Overview on page 72.

Outfeed Side The side of the table saw that the operator is farther from.

Panel Stock Any sheet stock that is used to decorate the walls of a home. Refer to Sheet Stock Overview on page 72 and Sawing a Raised Panel on pages 126 to 130.

Particleboard Sheet material made from wood chips or wood particles. Refer to Sheet Stock Overview on page 72.

Pitch Wood resin that develops on a circular-saw blade when it becomes hot. Refer to Removing Pitch on pages 45 and 46.

Plastic Laminates Material made when kraft paper and plastic resin are bonded under heat, and which serves as decorative and protective covers on sheet stock. Refer to Cutting Plastic Laminates on pages 113 to 116.

Rabbet An L-shaped channel that goes along the edge of a piece of stock. Refer to Rabbet Joints on pages 57 and 58 and Rabbets on pages 90 to 94.

Resawing The technique of ripping a thick piece of stock into two thinner pieces. Refer to Resawing on pages 110 to 112.

Retro-Fit Accessories Accessories that can be modified to be used with all table saws.

Rip Blade A blade with a straight-cutting edge that is designed to cut with the grain. Rip blades have deep gullets and large hook angles.

Rip Cut A cut made along the grain of the wood. Refer to Rip Cuts on pages 75 to 79.

Sheet Stock A term that refers to all wood material sold in sheets four feet wide and eight to twelve feet long. Common types of sheet stock include plywood, particleboard, hardboard, and paneling. Refer to Sheet Stock on page 72.

Sliding T Bevel A layout tool designed to lay out a bevel, a miter, or an angle.

Splitter A component on the table saw that holds the saw kerf open while cutting proceeds. Refer to Guard on pages 18 to 20.

Tear-out A condition in which the blade rips or tears out the grain of a workpiece. Tear-out can occur on the back, top, or bottom of a workpiece.

Tenoning Jig A commercial or user-made accessory designed to hold stock in a vertical or near-vertical orientation. Refer to Tenoning Jig on page 31.

Throat Plate (Table or Blade Insert)

The part of the table saw that covers the opening in the table that allows access to the arbor and splitter-mounting bracket. Refer to Throat Plate on page 22.

Tooth Set The bend in the blade's teeth that allows the blade to cut a kerf that is larger than the blade's thickness.

True Stock Stock with an edge and face perpendicular to each other.

Try Square A tool used to mark right angles on stock and also to check a corner to determine if it has been cut squarely.

Universal Jig A commercial or user-made accessory that is designed to hold stock in a vertical or near-vertical orientation or to hold irregularly shaped pieces.

Variety Saw *See* Bench Saw

Vibration A condition in which the table-saw blade shakes when cutting. A vibrating blade will make an uneven cut. See Minimizing Vibration on page 35.

METRIC EQUIVALENTS CHART

INCHES TO MILLIMETERS AND CENTIMETERS

MM— Millimeters   CM—Centimeters

Inches	MM	CM	Inches	CM	Inches	CM
⅛	3	0.3	9	22.9	30	76.2
¼	6	0.6	10	25.4	31	78.7
⅜	10	1.0	11	27.9	32	81.3
½	13	1.3	12	30.5	33	83.8
⅝	16	1.6	13	33.0	34	86.4
¾	19	1.9	14	35.6	35	88.9
⅞	22	2.2	15	38.1	36	91.4
1	25	2.5	16	40.6	37	94.0
1¼	32	3.2	17	43.2	38	96.5
1½	38	3.8	18	45.7	39	99.1
1¾	44	4.4	19	48.3	48	101.6
2	51	5.1	20	50.8	41	104.1
2½	64	6.4	21	53.3	42	106.7
3	76	7.6	22	55.9	43	109.2
3½	89	8.9	23	58.4	44	111.8
4	102	10.2	24	61.0	45	114.3
4½	114	11.4	25	63.5	46	116.8
5	127	12.7	25	66.0	47	119.4
6	152	15.2	27	68.6	48	121.9
7	178	17.8	28	71.1	49	124.5
8	203	20.3	29	73.7	50	127.0

Index